No Quarter November

No Quarter November

THE ANTHOLOGY

DOUGLAS WILSON

canonpress
Moscow, Idaho

Published by Canon Press
P.O. Box 8729, Moscow, ID 83843
800.488.2034 | www.canonpress.com

Douglas Wilson, *No Quarter November: The Anthology*
Copyright © 2019 by Douglas Wilson.

Printed in the United States of America.
Cover design by James Engerbretson.

Library of Congress Cataloging-in-Publication Data

Wilson, Douglas, 1953- author.
No quarter November : the anthology / Douglas Wilson.
Moscow : Canon Press, 2019.
LCCN 2019011213 | ISBN 9781947644878 (pbk. : alk. paper)
LCSH: Christianity--21st century. | Church. | Christianity and
   culture.
LCC BR481 .W55 2019 | DDC 277.3/083--dc23
LC record available at https://lccn.loc.gov/2019011213

19 20 21 22 23 24 25 26   10 9 8 7 6 5 4 3 2 1

To the burning couch crew.
You know who you are.

Contents

Introduction

So it is apparent that I believe that there really is a time for rhetorical qualifications. That time was not November 2018.

Allow me to explain. No, no, I insist. During the course of the month of November, my plan was to write a series of blog posts where I said what I think, flat out, and to do so without qualifying anything. The things I would write could potentially be qualified, and it would be no sin to do so, but my plan was to let everybody all know what was going on out there without any of that "but on the other hand" stuff. There is another hand with five fingers on it, and there are qualifications to be made, and you can rest assured that I knew all about them, but decided to keep them to myself.

This was kind of like a wordsmithing Mardi Gras. Or what happens in November stays in November.

For some reason, this whole thing reminds of a particular definition from Ambrose Bierce's *The Devil's Dictionary*:

EXILE, n. One who serves his country by residing abroad, yet is not an ambassador."

An English sea-captain being asked if he had read "The Exile of Erin," replied: "No, sir, but I should like to anchor on it." Years afterwards, when he had been hanged as a pirate after a career of unparalleled atrocities, the following memorandum was found in the ship's log that he had kept at the time of his reply: Aug. 3d, 1842. Made a joke on the ex-Isle of Erin. Coldly received. War with the whole world!

CHAPTER ONE

Burn All the Schools

H.L. Mencken once suggested a shrewd educational reform that has somehow not caught on. He said that there was nothing wrong with our current education establishment that could not be fixed by burning all the schools, and hanging all the teachers. Now some might want to dismiss this as an extreme measure, but visionaries are often dismissed in their own day. "You may say I'm a dreamer, but I'm not the only one . . . ."

Get Them Out Now

I do have an idea, followed by a question. Millions of evangelicals still have their children in the government school system. *Get them out now.* Having Christian children in the government school system is what theologians of another era would have called sinnity-sin-sin.

3

Not a little smidge of sinnity either.[1] Not really a debatable matter. Stop it. Crash the system. If there ever were to be a true reformation among us, Christians leaving the public school system would form a refugee column that would make the Mississippi River look like a solitary tear running down Horace Mann's cheek.

My question is a simple one, but I will divide it into two questions in just a moment. Here is the first phase of the question:

In order for all Christians to get their kids out of the maw of this government school system, what *would* it take precisely? How many outrages would have to be slathered over the tops of all of our heads before we said something like, "Friend, enough"? How outrageous would such outrages have to get before somebody noticed? How much before *everybody* noticed?

How far down this wormhole do we have to go?

Some time, away in the *future*, the last holdout, some Baptist deacon in Tennessee, will finally acknowledge that when the public school system refused to allow his (politely worded) request for his daughter to opt out of the lab for the pole dancing class, with the football team as the practice audience, they really had "gone too far." The football team was there because *they* were all in mandatory sensitivity training, which meant that they had to watch the girls without any catcalling, which they did grumble about a little bit.

Here is how the question divides. What it would take in 2018 is a very different question than what it will take twenty years from now, in 2038. The reason I know this is because what it would have taken in 1998, and before that in 1978, is quite different from what it would take now. Decadence, as Augustine once put it, is a conveyor

---

1. Now when I say . . . *Nope. You said you wouldn't. November, man.* Don't want people to think . . . *Doesn't matter what they think. If they are in sin anyway, all the qualifications in the world are just being pushed up the wrong rain spout.* Well, didn't feel like it anyway. *Good.* Sorry about that. Old habits die hard. *No problem.*

belt that has no off switch. Things that pass without comment today would have *caused riots* forty years ago. And that which would cause riots today is what you are prepping your great-grandchildren to put up with.

If you boil a frog slowly enough, as the adage has it, he will let you do it. If they are evangelical frogs, you can boil the whole Nile, with all of them in it. On a summer evening you can hear them croaking their praise choruses.

Can anybody imagine a school in 1958 where drag queens were in charge of the library reading hour? Can anybody imagine John Knox writing a stern letter to the school board about it, and speaking in opposition for his allotted three minutes at the public hearing that was scheduled for it? While you are at it, try to imagine him going up to the lectern with mincing step and simpering into the microphone.

The Heart of Our Compromise

This is the diseased heart of our great compromise. This is the Baal-grove out in front of Gideon's house. The sound of revival would be the sound of multiple chain saws firing up. If it doesn't smell like burning oil, and if it doesn't sound like those chain saws, it isn't revival.

Get them out now.

> So you, son of man, I have made a watchman for the house of Israel. Whenever you hear a word from my mouth, you shall give them warning from me. If I say to the wicked, O wicked one, you shall surely die, and you do not speak to warn the wicked to turn from his way, that wicked person shall die in his iniquity, but his blood I will require at your hand. But if you warn the wicked to turn from his way, and he does not turn from his way, that person shall die in his iniquity, but you will have delivered your soul. (Ezek. 33:7–9, ESV)

How many pastors have watched how many covenant children turned over to the godless so that the godless might oversee their growth and formation, and have *said nothing?* Pastors are those who must give an account. Part of giving an account means counting (Heb. 13:7, 17). So what is the casualty rate? How many survive that cliff you make them dive off? Any notion at all?

Yeah, I know. Some do survive. And those who survive can be pretty impressive, or pretty lucky, or both. And I know that there are Christian schools that barely merit the name, but *that* is nothing to the purpose. If I objected to an argument that urged us to send one hundred children through the Sunday Schools run by the JWs, along with a proud display of the three of them who made it, whose Trinitarianism was actually *strengthened* by the experience, it would still be a really lame argument.

If we were instructed to bring up our children in the nurture and admonition of the Lord (Eph. 6:4), if we were summoned to teach them the law of God in its fullness and to do so in a context entirely dominated by the entirety of the Word of God (Deut. 6:4-9), what good does it do to point at all the inconsistencies of people who have figured out creative ways of disobeying this? What is that to you? Get them out now.

What some people call having their children be salt and light, I call conscripting covenant children into becoming child soldiers, with all the grief that such recruitments entail. It makes me think of Dylan's *Thunder on the Mountain*—

> Gonna raise me an army, some tough sons of bitches
> I'll recruit my army from the orphanages

The orphans that *survive* fight well. So? Government schools are institutions controlled by the fatherless, staffed by the fatherless, with curriculum written by the fatherless, and attended by evangelical children who are functionally fatherless. I have known a number of such fathers who have big views of fatherhood, or so they think, but their vision for fatherhood is that biological function they share with donkeys and dogs. When fatherhood begins is one thing, but what it *entails* is quite another.

Get them out now.

CHAPTER TWO

Smash the Matriarchy

When I was a young boy, our family didn't own a television, which is why I was robbed of enjoying some of the greater cultural achievements of the mid-to-late-1950s. But as luck would have it, from time to time I did get a glimpse of some of those achievements, here and there on the run, you know. One time we were visiting some friends in another state, as I remember, and *they* had a television.

On this privileged occasion, I recall taking in an episode of *The Lone Ranger*. The theme of this particular show was about that time when there was this mousy little man, hen-pecked to the outer limits of human endurance, and through a series of circumstances, the Lone Ranger adopted this poor man and made him something of a protégé. The end result of this crash course in masculinity was that the little man headed on home, and the happy ending to the whole saga was him pulling out his revolver and shooting his wife's dishes off her shelves. It makes me happy just thinking about it. Fade to black, and with her thinking something along the lines of *finally!*

Now I know what you are thinking. You are thinking that this would be an excellent time for me to bend my "no qualifications" rule for November. No, not that. No qualifications. Fire away.

Or perhaps you were thinking that watching stuff like that must have been what turned an innocent little boy with a cute smile into the raging misogynist that he is today. No, that's not right either. My "raging misogyny" has other sources entirely.

Here's the right answer—or rather, here's what you *should* be thinking. You should be thinking that we are so far gone as a nation that we don't even recognize how much healthier that time was, shot up dishes and all. We like to flatter ourselves, saying that we have made "a lot of progress" on women's issues, while some of the more conservative among us lament the "side effects" of such progress, such as 60 million dead babies. But think for a moment. When I was watching that show, abortion was against the law in all fifty states. Maybe we have not progressed at all. Maybe the word for it is regress, or more accurately, apostasy.

About That Word *Matriarchy*

When I urge, as it appears I did in the title of this piece, the smashing of the matriarchy, I want to make sure to begin by defining our terms. This I propose to do, taking as my starting point a definition of matriarchy that runs thus: "a system of society or government ruled by a woman or women." But an adjustment is needed. A slight difficulty is caused by the fact that rule by mothers and rule by women are not necessarily the same thing. The word matriarchy has *mater* (mother) at the root, and so what could you call rule by women who have waged a very bloody war on the very idea of motherhood? It has been bloody enough to actually warrant the name of a monstrous regiment.

So whatever is happening, we are not actually being ruled by fruitful women (a state of affairs that *fruitful* women actually detest), but rather by men with a homosexual ethos who have recruited a horde of childless and gullible women to serve as their honey-trap shock troops. Such women are those who have accepted the flattering vanities of career "advancement" in place of a truly satisfying life as the active mother of a teeming and energetic pack of yard apes. These duped women have somehow been persuaded that the good opinion of the bureaucrats in HR is somehow far more valuable than the good opinion of the yard apes. It isn't, by the way.

Unfortunately, we don't have a word for rule by that sort of women. We don't have a word for "rule by barren feminists who have been snookered by the homosexual vibe," so *matriarchy* will have to do as a stand-in for the present. But it is a stipulated definition, and the true nature of it will be revealed in due course.

Cut to the Chase

The gifts that make women such a marvel and wonder are not those gifts which equip them for rule. Women are not supposed to rule over men because they are, generally speaking, taking one thing with another, no good at it.

There are three basic governments that God has established among men, and according to Scripture women are restricted from rule in all three of them. In two of these governments, the restriction is general, and in one it is absolute. We shall consider each one in turn.

But be aware of this. Going into it, if you grant the ethic validity of the feminist definition of "sexism," then it follows necessarily that the Bible is a sexist book, needing to be rejected or adjusted. Such attempts at least have the virtue of consistency. But what are we to do with those evangelical leaders who claim that the Bible is the very Word of *God*, and who then make all their adjustments on the sly?

Let us start with the absolute restriction. Women may not exercise authority over men in the authority structure of the church (1 Tim. 2:12; 1 Cor. 14:34). And this is not supposed to be taken by us as one of those inexplicable and insane restrictions that God placed on us in order to test our faith. No, it is not the case that women would make great pastors, and God arbitrarily said that we weren't supposed to do it anyway. No, Paul gives us *reasons* why women are not to rule in the Church—one theological and one practical. The theological reason is that if women rule in the Church this is plainly an attempt to invert the creation order. God made Adam first, and then Eve (1 Tim. 2:13). The man was not made for the woman, but the woman for the man (1 Cor. 11:8-9). And the practical reason is that if women rule, given the fact that they are more likely to be deceived, this means they are more likely to pass such deceptions on to the congregation. That would be, according to the apostle, "not very good."

Second, in the government of the household, the Scripture requires women to be submissive, in subjection, and obedient. "Wives, *submit yourselves* unto your own husbands, as unto the Lord" (Eph. 5:22; emphasis added) "Likewise, ye wives, *be in subjection* to your own husbands; that, if any obey not the word, they also may without the word be won by the conversation of the wives" (1 Pet. 3:1; emphasis added). "To be discreet, chaste, keepers at home, good, *obedient to their own husbands*, that the word of God be not blasphemed" (Tit. 2:5; emphasis added).

The dilemma underneath the word rendered in these places as *submissive*, *in subjection*, and *obedient to* is a word that—once we have soaked it overnight in a pan of rancid zeitgeistian assumptions, and pounded it for half an hour with the meat mallet of eisegetical hubris—is surprisingly elastic. *Now* the original word actually means spunky, full of sass, street smart, independent, brassy, saucy, large and in charge. Much as the Greek word for head, *kephale*, actually means the curly little tails that piglets have, so also the word that our versions mistakenly render as *obedient* here is a word that actually means *worthy of receiving obedience*. Why, we have gotten the whole picture upside down!

And incidentally, if anyone requires further proof that women shouldn't be teachers—because they are so easily deceived—then look no further than the widespread acceptance of this exegetical putrescence among them. If someone points out that there are men who accept these insights too, the response should be, yeah, well, they shouldn't be teachers either.

And what about civil government? Scripture describes the curse that a land suffers under when women are running the show. More on why this is the case below.

"As for my people, children are their oppressors, and women rule over them. O my people, they which lead thee cause thee to err, and destroy the way of thy paths" (Is. 3:12). Isaiah is describing Israel in quite a sorry state, struggling along under a curse placed upon them by God. When a nation defaults to leadership from the immature (who are not ready for rule) or from women (who were not created for rule), the end results are not at all good.

So women were not designed for rule. They are forbidden to rule in the Church. They are forbidden to rule their husbands at home. And they are not supposed to rule over Israel in such a way as to "cause her to err," destroying their paths.

The Complementarian Cave-In

It is *de rigueur* among conservatish and complementarianish commentators to say things like "it is true that" a woman cannot be a pastor, although said commentator knows many women who could be *outstanding* pastors. And they go on to say that on those *rare* instances when the marriage vote keeps coming up a tie, the husband gets to—reluctantly, with a tear in his eye and an ache in his heart—break the tie. Both husband and wife promised during pre-marriage counseling to tell none of their friends if this ever happens.

I used the phrase *de rigueur* just now to describe this vibe, but that sounds too much like *rigorous*, which creates the wrong impression entirely. Nothing about any of this is rigorous. Still we have to use the words available.

So what the complementarian consensus appears to be is this: the entire world can be shaped into just the configuration that the radical feminists demand, with women staffing SWAT teams, landing on aircraft carriers, playing football, singing bass, you-name-it, and stalwart Christians can still be faithful (*honest*) if they manage to hang onto a couple of private reserves, each one of them suitably small. They will (for now) keep her out of the pulpit that adorns the sanctuary of their private little mystery religion. In addition, they also think they can be faithful if they limit their authority/submission thing in marriage to the privacy of their own *home*, kind of like those times when he pretends to be a surgeon and she pretends to be an ER nurse.

The Knowledge of Good and Evil

What is the source of all this foolishness? If we want to know why our generation is spending so much time listening to the serpent, we will have to go back to the Garden. Believe it or not, there is some information there.

"But the tree of the knowledge of good and evil, thou shalt not eat of it: for in the day that thou eatest thereof thou shalt surely die" (Gen. 2:17).

"But strong meat belongeth to them that are of full age, even those who by reason of use have their senses exercised to discern both good and evil" (Heb. 5:14).

We should all know that there was one prohibited tree in the Garden of Eden, the tree of knowledge of good and evil. The tree of life was not prohibited (Gen. 2:16), but once sin had entered the world it went off limits—lest we should eat from it in a rebellious condition and live forever that way, unredeemable (Gen. 3:22, 24). So God in His mercy barred the way back to the tree of life, until it was opened up again in and through the gospel (Rev. 2:7).

But what about the tree of the knowledge of good and evil? What *was* it?

So we need to take a moment to consider what that phrase means, and what it does not mean.

Now "the knowledge of good and evil" cannot mean experience of sin. The Lord Himself said that *He* had that knowledge—"Behold, the man is become *as one of us*, to know good and evil" (Gen. 3:22; emphasis added). The serpent earlier had promised that this knowledge would make them "as God" (or gods), "knowing good and evil" (Gen. 3:5). Millennia later, the author of Hebrews does not identify this ability to distinguish sin from righteousness as

experience of sin in itself, but rather with maturity, with the capacity
to handle "strong meat."

Too many Christians assume that a pre-fall lack of the knowledge
of good and evil was a total blank innocence, no ethical categories at
all. But if this were the case then how would Adam have been able
to fall into sin? How would he have known it was evil to eat from the
prohibited tree? No, the knowledge of good and evil here *has to mean
something more* than a simple knowledge of the difference between
right and wrong.

So what is it then? What did Eve reach for? What was she deceived about?

The issue was rule. God had created mankind to rule over creation and all creatures (Gen. 1:27-30). In learning how to judge and
rule the created order, man really would be like God (Eccl. 12:14).
Entering into that rule would have been a transition from immatu-
rity to maturity, and not a transition from moral cluelessness into an
ability to tell right from wrong. Kings make judgments. They have to
be able to discern right and wrong in the case before them.

Now it is quite true that the Bible often speaks of "good" and
"evil" in the simple moral categories of individuals learning to love
the good and hate what is evil. But when we talk about *this* kind of
discernment for rule, we are talking about the ability to tell good
from almost good, to discern the difference between white and off-
white. Because God created us for rule, He created us for this. And
when our first parents ate this forbidden fruit, they were grabbing
for such rule prematurely, before God gave it to them as a gift.

This is what Eve did, and this is what she persuaded her husband
to do.

In discussing this kind of rule, we are talking about what little children don't do, and what kings are called to do. Consider the language

of Scripture on this. "Moreover your little ones, which ye said should be a prey, and your children, which in that day had *no knowledge between good and evil*, they shall go in thither . . ." (Deut. 1:39; emphasis added, cf. Jer. 4:22). This was true of a type of the Messiah, the child born in fulfillment of the promise to Isaiah. "Behold a virgin shall conceive, and bear a son, and shall call his name Immanuel . . . for before the child shall *know to refuse the evil, and choose the good*, the land that thou abhorrest shall be forsaken of both her kings" (Is. 7:14-16; emphasis added). In a similar way, extreme old age prevents a man from being able to serve as a judge between good and evil, as Barzillai observed: "I am this day fourscore years old: and can I *discern between good and evil* . . .?" (2 Sam. 19:35; emphasis added).

And how did Solomon please the Lord when a vision was given to him at Gibeon? Even though he sacrificed in the high places, he did love the Lord (1 Kgs. 3:3). When the Lord appeared to Solomon in a dream and told him to ask for whatever he would have, Solomon's answer pleased the Lord (1 Kgs. 3:10). So what did Solomon ask for? He said first that he was "but a little child" (1 Kgs. 3:7), and so what deficiency did he think needed to be corrected? "Give therefore thy servant an understanding heart to judge thy people, *that I may discern between good and bad*: for who is able to judge this thy so great a people" (1 Kings 3:10; emphasis added)?

We are called to understand the world so that we might grow up into a maturity that is capable of ruling the world. The author of Hebrews knows and understands the creation mandate. He quotes Psalm 8 in this regard, and says that we do not yet see everything subject to mankind—but we do see Jesus (Heb. 2:9). The world to come is not subject to angels, but to mankind (Heb. 2:5ff). Mankind in Christ is therefore being fitted for godly rule (Heb. 5:14). Because we grabbed the forbidden fruit out of order, we have needed to be retro-fitted for it, but this is what is happening.

Let us bring all this back then to Eve. Scripture is very plain that she was deceived.

"But I fear, lest by any means, as the serpent beguiled Eve through his subtilty, so your minds should be corrupted from the simplicity that is in Christ" (2 Cor. 11:3).

But what was the *point* of the deception? Eve thought that she was grasping the ability to rule, and she went first, going ahead of her husband. She persuaded him to come behind her, but what she thought she was doing was entering into rule. The fruit was pleasant to look upon, and it was delicious, but the real draw was in the fact that she would be as the gods, "knowing good and evil" (Gen. 3:5). So what did she think she was reaching for? Her interpretation was that the tree was one to "be desired to make one wise" (Gen. 3:6). Wisdom for what? To do what? To make judgments, to *rule*. Centuries later, John calls the third element in this triadic temptation the "pride of life" (1 Jn. 2:16). This usurpation, and Adam's subsequent ratification of it, lies at the base of all our woes.

Mankind, man and woman together, had already been given dominion over all the creatures (Gen. 1:26-27). But because this was not enough for them, and because they prematurely reached for a greater rule than what had been given, what happened? Instead of the created order flourishing under him, Adam faced a world that would be far less cooperative (Gen. 3:17-19). And because Eve wanted rule so badly, part of her unhappy lot was to *be* ruled. Her desire for rule backfired.

"Unto the woman he said, I will greatly multiply thy sorrow and thy conception; in sorrow thou shalt bring forth children; and thy desire shall be to thy husband, *and he shall rule over thee*" (Gen. 3:16; emphasis added).

The Actual State of Affairs

When God cursed the ground for Adam's benefit, He was not making suggestions for the ground to follow—suggestions that the ground might or might not want to listen to. The ground was simply cursed. When God multiplied the sorrows of childbirth for the woman, and when He said that the woman would be ruled, this was also a statement of fact. This was just the way it was going to be.

And so what this means is that when women rule, as is happening in our day, something else is going on. When feminism is in the ascendant, this means that we are actually being ruled by the (male) manipulators behind them. When women rule, this actually means that (wicked) men are ruling, with women being used as their instrument.

God has configured the world in such a way that males will be dominant. Nothing whatever can be done about that. But because sin is a reality, such dominance will either be constructive or destructive, obedient to God or disobedient to God. And what feminism does is outlaw constructive male dominance. And what happens when you outlaw constructive male dominance? Only outlaws will have dominance. And so feminism is actually an ideology that paves the way for the rule of wicked men. This "empowerment" of women is actually one more deception of women, in a long list of deceptions, and, like always, it leaves them miserable.

Explain to us again why women, having been liberated, need to be so heavily medicated?

The Voice of the Serpent

Someone (I am sure) will want to say that all that I have described is a result of the Fall, and that Christ came in order to reverse the consequences of the Fall, did He not? In the redemption offered by Christ there is neither Jew nor Greek, male or female, etc.

Whatever reversals of the Fall might be contained in the glorious redemption of Christ, they will *not* be mediated to us through the voice of the serpent. The serpent beguiled Eve through "subtlety," and Paul was worried that the Corinthians were displaying an analogous gullibility.

He was worried about the kind of gullibility, in fact, that is on high display today among what might be called chump-evangelicals. So if your pastor no longer includes the promise "to obey" as part of the bride's vow in the weddings he performs, he is listening to the voice of the serpent. If your pastor thinks it a matter of scriptural indifference whether women are brought into combat roles (Deut. 22:5), he is listening to the voice of the serpent. If your pastor will not address characteristic feminine temptations from the pulpit, he is listening to the voice of the serpent. If your pastor is "woke" on gender issues, he is listening to the voice of the serpent. If your pastor teaches that masculine authority is only "a thing" in the sacred two square feet behind the pulpit, and in the private, oh, so private decisions that a husband and wife might make together in the *privacy* of their own homes, he is listening to the voice of the serpent.

It is hard to escape the conclusion that most of the evangelical world is doing exactly that.

And actually, "listening to the voice of the serpent" is kind of the best-case scenario. Worst case is that such men *are* the voice of the serpent.

CHAPTER THREE

Horny Presbyterians and Woke Baptists

Mamas, Don't Let Your Babies Grow Up to Be Preachers

Mothers naturally want their children to be safe, and to remain safe throughout the course of their lives. But wise mothers don't value that safety above all things. Better to be the mother of a son who dies valiantly in battle than the mother of a coward who lives long— "come back with your shield or on it" really is a noble sentiment.

So in a time of hot persecution, there is a natural affection that would certainly tempt a mother to want her son to "stay safe," which would mean staying out of front line ministry. This is a natural inclination, and it must be mortified. But there is also a love for God— in days like ours when cowardice is deemed cool—that should *prevent* mothers from wanting their sons in *that* kind of ministry. Why should she want him to be preeminent among all the woke cowards?

So, as already indicated, we are living in just such a time, which is why mamas shouldn't want their babies to grow up to be preachers—at least the kind of preachers who have learned how to rebuke "sin" (now known as human flourishing deficit points) through six or seven layers of homiletical cotton wool. *Woomfy woomf fuflowy!* The word of God preached *right* is sharper than a two-edged sword, separating the joints and marrow (Heb. 4:12). The word of God mumbled in a way that comports with aforesaid human flourishing is like swatting some tank of a badly-behaving toddler, delivering what sounded like a decisive *whomp* on top of his diaper *and* overalls. *That'll* show him.

How Is This Possible?

So how is it possible for America to be so corrupt, as corrupt as she has become, and for us to have so many millions of evangelical believers, and to have so many thousands of men preaching to all of us, week after week, and not have hundreds of those men in jail? I am referring to men being jailed, not for throwing bombs, but for preaching the kind of sermons that matter.

How is it that our sermons present so little of a threat that they can be for the most part ignored?

"In your struggle against sin you have not yet resisted to the point of shedding your blood." (Heb. 12:4, ESV).

God created the world through the Word (Jn. 1:1). He spoke and it came to be. God recreated the world, giving us a new heavens and new earth, and He did so through the Word. The Word became flesh and dwelt among us (Jn. 1:14). The Word then gave His apostles the ministry of subduing the world through the preached Word, and this was a mission that they passed on to their preaching successors (Matt. 28:19-20), which ought to include us. So in line with all that, we should be men who preach like howitzers in the field, and yet the effect nowadays is more like powder puff cannons in the circus.

The Nature of Our Cowardice

We are in a hot war, and yet we somehow have come to think it is actually an occasion for sitting on our kindergarten carpet squares in order to learn from the nice lady how not to run with scissors. Whenever somebody pulls off some fresh new outrage, we think it is sufficient to assure people who ask us about it that we firmly "disagree." Oh, so glad you "disagree." So we are all done then? We can then wait around patiently for the next theological atrocity so we can differ with that one also? Just so long as you *differ*. Just so long as you keep your own nose clean.

Comes now a Lutheran pastor lady who assures us that the use of porn is just fine, especially if the porn is "ethically sourced." She has a book coming out soon, and because God loves to lay the irony on thick, it is entitled *Shameless*.

"But I have this against you, that you tolerate that woman Jezebel, who calls herself a prophetess and is teaching and seducing my servants to practice sexual immorality and to eat food sacrificed to idols" (Rev. 2:20, ESV).

What does Jesus hate about you Lutherans? This is not a trick question. He hates how *tolerant* you are. That *virtue* you celebrate? That tolerance that you think is so fine? Jesus hates it, because, as all Bible readers know, Jesus is a hater.

Jesus hated the same thing about the Corinthians. They had a guy in their congregation who was getting it on with his stepmom, and certain woke Corinthians were *proud* of their go-along, get-along attitude about it.

"It is actually reported that there is sexual immorality among you, and of a kind that is not tolerated even among pagans, for a man has his father's wife. And you are arrogant! Ought you not rather to mourn? Let him who has done this be removed from among you." (1 Cor. 5:1-2, ESV).

But the Lord takes a dim view of all those rainbow decals. When the elements melt with a fervent heat, all of them are going to peel right off.

Now how hard would it be to find Lutherans who "disagreed" with the Rev. Porn-Lady's approach? Not hard at all. Her approach to porn would have to be considered "problematic," at least in some quarters. It certainly is "distressing." Not a few are sick about it. It is also *tolerated*, by the way. We don't need to look hard to find somebody who "differs" with this kind of thing. We do need somebody to put their foot through the side of it.

Yeah, but what Wilson apparently does not know is that this lady is from a *mainline* denomination. Everybody knows how messed up the mainlines are. All of us know that. That is a given. That is granted.

Where the mainline denominations came from is still a grand mystery, it appears.

All of the mainlines were at one time—within living memory—evangelical denominations, and slowly, imperceptibly, magically, inexorably, *something* happened, we know not what. These things just occur, and we can't stop it from happening. If only we knew what was causing it!

Over the last two centuries, so many denominations, seminaries, magazines, universities, publishing houses, etc. have gone liberal *that you would think that we knew what it looked like by now.* Unlike the mercies of God, which are new every morning, the devil's tricks are always the same. Why should he change anything up, when the same trick always does the trick?

Look, friends. This rot, this cancer, this corruption, this gangrene, this contagion, this oozing blister, has already settled down for a long stay in the two most influential evangelical denominations in America—the PCA and the SBC—and unless somebody does something different, the whole inexorable process is going to go exactly the same way. We therefore currently have two kinds of denominations in America—we have the mainlines and we have the future mainlines.

Note to anyone paying attention, on the off-chance that somebody out there *is* paying attention: There is a difference between "differing" and *doing* something "different." In principle, the evangelical (for now) Presbyterians are sunk because of sex and the evangelical (for now) Baptists are sunk because of race. The progressives placed their torpedoes in different places in their respective hulls. The torpedoes did come from different directions—one from the northeast and one from the southwest, but the ships are both headed in the same direction, which is to say, toward Davy Jones.

The Presbyterians let *Revoice* sail right on into their New Jerusalem, bringing them apes, ivory and peacocks from the distant land of Oprah, and the Baptists are getting themselves racially woke. And if there is anything worse than a horny Presbyterian, it would have to be a woke Baptist. Know what I'm saying?

CHAPTER FOUR

Evolution as an Uncommonly Silly Idea

Prolegomena to the Skylarking

One of the things a writer must do, if he is planning on running with the big boys, is demonstrate his erudition and learning as he starts off the proceedings, and to do so by means of judicious citations. What better way to set the tone than by quoting the trenchant expertise of others? And because I am going to be tackling a view held by virtually all the real brains of the scientific world, that ratio being settled by the Credentials Office of the Cartel, who better to cite than a business management consultant and a journalist?

Peter Drucker once made this observation, one that holds true outside the world of business, out to the edge of the universe in fact: "The only things that evolve by themselves in an organization are disorder, friction, and malperformance."[2]

2 Peter Drucker, *Management: Tasks, Responsibilities, Practices* (Oxford: Butterworth Heinemann, 1974), 444.

And Malcolm Muggeridge, no slouch when it came to astute observation, once said this: "I myself am convinced that the theory of evolution, especially to the extent to which it has been applied, will be one of the greatest jokes in the history books of the future. Posterity will marvel that so very flimsy and dubious an hypothesis could be accepted with the incredible credulity it has."[3]

Actual Introduction

The initial presenting problem is how and why highly intelligent people can believe and do extraordinarily foolish things. We see this in day-to-day sorts of situations, as when a very smart woman makes obviously bad romantic choices, or when a statistician, who actually knows the actual odds, throws a bunch of money away in some gambling spree. A shiny hot car can have a superb engine, along with a tachometer that bounces crazily on the right side of the dial, and still be on the wrong road.

This has corporate and societal applications also. In the history of dumb ideas—we have agreed to speak frankly throughout the month of November—the gold and silver medalists would have to be Darwinism and Marxism. Marxism believes, for example, that it can cost a dollar to make a loaf of bread, and that we can make everybody sell it for 50 cents a loaf, and yet, at the end of the day, still have bread. This is tantamount to believing that 3 is bigger than 5, and yet the fact remains that the people who actually *believe* this are clustered in our major universities. You know, our grand societal thinkery-spots.

And Darwinism! But I must restrain myself. Don't want to get out over the fronts of my skis. Gotta pace myself here.

3 Malcolm Muggeridge, The Advocate (March 1984): 7.

Set the Stage

Spider webs that are marvels of structural engineering, millions of them all over the globe, made by spiders with the intelligence of an arachnid with a teeny little brain . . . not to mention the intelligence of a trained structural engineer. Migratory Arctic terns which fly from Antarctica to the Arctic and back again, mysteriously finding their way each way. Eons ago one bright tern said to another one, "You know, given the tilt of the earth's axis, I'll bet it is summer on the other end of this globe when it is winter here . . . you know?" And because one good tern deserves another, the two of them set off, and eventually persuaded all the others that this was the way to enjoy endless summer. Then there are the beetles, over three hundred thousand *species* of beetles, careening around in the backyards of who knows how many of us. Salt water salmon heading up fresh water rivers in order to spawn, letting nothing whatever interfere with their urgent need to get there. Monarch butterflies, which have never been to the particular spot in Mexico where they all spend the winter, make a trek there by the millions. Trillions of cells in one human body, each one of them orders of magnitude finer than an exquisite watch, all of them synchronized and working together. Then consider a particular kind of caterpillar, which when frightened by a predatory bird, has a rear end that swells up into the shape of a venomous viper head. Another butterfly, bright blue when its wings are spread, folds them up together to look for all the world like a brown, dried-up leaf. Down at the microscopic level, DNA replicates itself like it was a factory filled with exquisitely-tuned robotic machines. Another insect, stumbling onto the aforementioned dried leaf strategy by blind, stupid, purposeless chance, looks exactly like a different kind of dried up leaf. Blind impersonal forces really enjoy that dried leaf trick. Protein chains fold up elegantly, just like that garden hose in your shed over the winter that doesn't ever get tangled. Oh, your hoses *do* get tangled? You must not be trained in science.

And then keep in mind the fact that I have listed here a small handful of marvels, which when compared to all the marvels which *could* be listed, are like one little tiny BB, rolling around on the concrete floor of an empty CostCo warehouse.

What do you get when you take a "just so" story, and multiply it to the 178th power? You get the assured results of *science*, you fundamentalist ninny-hammer, and why aren't you bowing down to the sound of the cornet, flute, dulcimer, and sackbut?

Dullards, Dogberry, and Darwin

A common emphasis among Christians is that folly, biblically defined, is *not* the same thing as stupidity. We are told, *ad nauseam*, that biblical folly is a *moral* category, not an intellectual one. It is claimed that a fool in the biblical sense might do very well indeed on an IQ test. Moreover, since we are speaking frankly, my interlocutor might say, a fool in the biblical sense might run IQ circles around, as the Victorians might put it, the present writer. The present writer is perhaps standing out there on a wide flat surface of some pretty pedestrian assumptions about common sense science, as he probably *is*, while the bosses of the world spin scientific Brodies around him. Thus the narrative goes, as we are constantly cautioned to remember—we are dealing with very *smart* people.

So, we are assured, yet again, that when Scripture says something like, "The fool hath said in his heart, There is no God" (Ps. 14:1), . . . fool does not actually mean, you know, fool. The point is earnestly made that this is a *moral* folly, not an intellectual deficiency. Never, ever assume that unbelievers are operating foolishly in the intellectual realm. They are very smart people. If they were not smart people, how could we look up to them, yearn after them, and wish we could be like them? Well, that's foolish too, and it seems that we *are* becoming like them.

But the Scriptures teach us that such moral folly *results in* intellectual darkness. "*Having the understanding darkened*, being alienated from the life of God through the ignorance that is in them, because of the blindness of their heart" (Eph. 4:18; emphasis added). Where does the darkness of understanding come from? It comes from the blindness of their heart.

"Because that, when they knew God, they glorified him not as God, neither were thankful; but became vain in their imaginations, and their foolish heart was darkened" (Rom. 1:21). A refusal to honor God as God, and refusal to give Him thanks, results in what? Darkness of heart, and vanity of imagination.

So while it may be technically true, so far as it goes, that a smart person (by a stipulated and narrow set of measurements) can deny that God made the world and all that it contains, it remains the case that such a person is thereupon called upon to affirm, with a solemn countenance, a series of propositions that are stupid—and I mean stupid with three o's.

All this means is that a genius need not be dullard in order to be a fool. The fact that the fool is not brain-power rpm impaired simply means that his stupidity does not have an explanation that is located in his natural mental limitations. The stupidity—and it is very real stupidity—must therefore be coming from somewhere else. In fact, when the person involved is not mentally handicapped that actually makes the stupidity *more* stupid, not less.

If a simpleton assured you that wet streets cause rain, we can attribute the stupid claim to the stupidity of the source. But if a man with perfect GRE scores and three graduate degrees tells you the same thing, it remains stupid. In fact, the stupidity is compounded by the "ought-to-know-better" component, not diminished. And so as to keep our eye on the ball, to claim that a little yellow canary is a blood cousin to the sea lion is a more egregious howler than thinking wet streets cause rain.

The point I am building up to is this: Darwinism is not simply an error. It is not an understandable mistake. It is not a reasonable theory that has one unfortunate downside, that condition of happening not to be true. No, Darwinism is incoherent, disordered, and jumbled. It really is ludicrous, risible, and stupid. Moreover it is the kind of stupidity that rises to the greatest heights of stupidity, in that smart people are peculiarly attracted to it. What we call smart people are often very vain and conceited people, and they do not want God over them. And rather than submit to the wisdom of God, they will go for *anything*.

"For since, in the wisdom of God, the world did not know God through wisdom, it pleased God through the folly of what we preach to save those who believe" (1 Cor. 1:21, ESV). Their wisdom is our folly, and vice versa.

The apostle Paul once said that the sins of some men go before them, while the sins of others come behind (1 Tim. 5:24). The same thing goes for stupidity. When someone like Dogberry does his thing, everybody can see it, right out there in the open. It goes before him: "One word, sir. Our watch, sir, have indeed *comprehended* two *aspicious* persons, and we would have them this morning examined before your worship.[4]

But when Sir Richard Houghton III says something like, "As Witherton demonstrated in his landmark study, the transitional

---

4 William Shakespeare, *Much Ado about Nothing*, Act 3, Scene 5.

forms between *Orcinus orca* and *Bos taurus* or *Bos indicus* would have to be considered to include, at a minimum, a diminutive form of *Lepus roseus*," our temptation of course is to go *whoa—that's some high-flying education right there.* But what he just said was that orca whales came from cows through the intermediate staging area of little pink bunnies, and that Witherton, who hasn't been locked up yet, also thinks the same thing. And yes, I know that actual evolutionary theory does not include the bunnies. I put those in to make the whole thing more realistic and down to earth, to keep from straining credulity to the breaking point. You know, to provide some verisimilitude. The cow > whale scenario needed *something* to keep us all from laughing out loud.

So Who Do You Think You Are?

So when I say that Darwinism is stupid—someone might interject— am I not setting myself up against the entire world of accepted and accredited learning? And not only have I done that, he continues, I have first called their science into question, and then I descended to personalities. I am not simply maintaining that Darwinism (happens to be) false, which is a serious thought crime in itself, but I am also maintaining that it is ludicrous, ridonkulous, preposterous, farcical, an *idée fixe thrown from the high cliffs of evidentiary knowledge onto the rocks of blinkered ignorance. And if I am asked for my authority to speak with such confidence on such things, I can produce . . . what? An MA in philosophy from the University of Idaho?*

Yup.

"I have more understanding than all my teachers: For thy testimonies are my meditation. I understand more than the ancients, because I keep thy precepts" (Ps. 119:99–100).

Kneel before Your Maker

The central problem is the conceit of man. Because of an establishment-wide ignorant pomposity, strictly enforced by tenure tribunals, it has become impossible to draw the most obvious of conclusions—which is that the Creator is an artistic engineer of infinite *majesty*.

"O come, let us worship and bow down: Let us *kneel* before the LORD our *maker*" (Ps. 95:6; emphasis added). Because the Lord is our *Maker*, the posture we should have before Him is that of *kneeling*. The secular evolutionist does not want to kneel, and therefore it is necessary for him to deny that he has a Maker. He can follow a logical argument to *that* extent. For if he had a Maker, kneeling is the obvious thing to do, and he is too proud to kneel. Too conceited to kneel. Too vain to kneel. Too puffed up to kneel. Too bloated with intellectual gasses emanating from his head to kneel.

Because he valued his mind over the glory of his Maker, this is the reason he has lost his mind. You would not have your God as God, and so it is that your cisterns can hold no water (Jer. 2:13), just like your arguments. He valued science over his Maker, and this is the reason he has lost most of his science already, and will lose the rest of it when he finally makes it to the outer darkness. Denying God does not just mean losing *God*. Denying God means that you also lose the thing you substituted in for Him.

If you substituted science for God, then you lose God, and your soul, *and* science along the way. More than that, worse than that, all the bumpkins that you used to look down on, despising them for their know-nothing approach to science, will come to know far more of real science than you do. You have done post-doc work at Oxford *and* Harvard, and the average graduate of Buffalo Breath Bible College knows more about what is going on in the natural world than you will ever know.

You do not know what you think you know. Because it is not well with your soul, your mind has become diseased and scarred. Your mind cannot bend in the right ways anymore, cannot bend to fit around the evidence, but the way to fix all that is to start with your knees. The *knees* have to bend first.

CHAPTER FIVE

PCA, RIP

Bear with me for just a few moments. This will get livelier, and a lot more interesting, in just short while.

I am not seeking to qualify my point, as should become apparent shortly, but I do need to state my qualifications to make the point. Those qualifications, as I hope you will acknowledge shortly, are sterling, and a central part of my argument. We are struggling with different definitions of the word *qualification* here. In speaking to this issue of the coming demise of the PCA, I have the qualifications to make no qualifications.

I am not a member of a PCA church, nor have I ever been a member of a PCA church. I grew up in Southern Baptist circles, and after my hitch in the Navy, found myself pastoring a Jesus-people-like baptistic fellowship. That church started to grow, and so I couldn't really get away to seminary. I finished my formal schooling in philosophy, and then turned to an OJT reading program in theology. As a result of books—a series of dangerous books—I began to career through some of my paradigm shifts, like I was a exegetical pinball or something. I started out a conservative evangelical of baptistic mien, and in the mid-eighties I became postmill. Then in 1988 I became a Calvinist. One thing led to another, and by 1993, I was a paedobaptist.

Me becoming a paedobaptist caused no little consternation on the session of our church, and so the elders began the process of removing me from the pulpit. We then had a heads of household meeting in which the congregation (still mostly baptists or agno-baptists) told the elders in no uncertain terms that they did not want to divide over this issue, and that they wanted the elders to work it out. After that crisis, the church did eventually come to a "baptismal cooperation agreement," which enabled our baptists, paedobaptists, and agno-baptists to work together.

The reason this is relevant is that it essentially cut off any real prospect of us joining a confessionally Reformed body like the OPC or PCA. We did send one delegation to a meeting of the Northwest Presbytery of the PCA, but nothing came of that. I did not want to join a historically Reformed body if the price of that admission was me double-crossing the baptists who had stood by me in our baptismal crisis/controversy. And so that brought in the Groucho Marx rule as applied to presbyteries—I didn't want to join one that would have us. I didn't want anyone to water down their standards on baptism (heh), and I also didn't want to desert the men who had stood with me.

So there we were, and that set the stage for the formation of the Communion of Reformed Evangelical Churches (CREC), which also accommodates differing views on baptism.

Yes, But . . .

Now I know that some of you may be looking at your watches. This seems like it should be filed under *that's-all-very-interesting-but*. Are you not simply tracing for us the very shadowy outlines of your fairly oblique connections with the PCA? And thus establishing for us the uncouthness of your rudeness in pronouncing a funeral oration—as it is apparent from the title of this post—over a body you never had anything to do with? How am I not taking a passing dog by the ears?

But here is the point, and it's a hummer. The PCA was formed in 1973, and I think it is safe to say that from that time down to the present, one of the biggest controversies that that denomination has ever gone through was the Federal Vision controversy. That controversy spanned many years, many presbyteries, and included pronouncements of the General Assembly. Numerous PCA men were charged with doctrinal heterodoxy in PCA courts (Leithart, Wilkins, Meyers, et al)—with varying results but with no one convicted of heresy. Conferences were held, books were published, phone calls were not returned, invitations to speak were withdrawn, anathemas were hurled, and so on. A Niagara of words poured over the lip of the falls. As said above, this was one of the biggest controversies, if not *the* biggest, the PCA has ever had.

And I was one of the central combatants in that fray. I was smack in the middle of it. That position gave me a peculiar vantage.

Most of my contributions to the polemical back and forth were published on my blog. I recently pulled all those posts together in one book, and the word count for that book came in northwards of 300,000 words. I had a great deal to say, and almost all of it was in response to what others were saying, usually pretty loudly. And those incoming accusations, many of them, most of them, were from the PCA.

And so here is my foundation premise, the one I want to argue from. Lick your pencil, and write this down.

I believe that no one in North America has a better grasp than I do on what it means to have the PCA deal with something or someone they consider a threat. I honestly think that I am the world's leading expert on this topic. No one knows better than I do what it looks like when the PCA swings into action to deal with something. On this one, I know my onions first hand.

The Mills of the Gods

Now I have heard from some good people in the PCA that the Revoice business *is* being attended to. The mills of the gods . . . exceeding fine . . . slow, painstaking . . . Presbyterians are all about process . . . patience, patience, *patience*.

Excuse me, and please see above. I know how the PCA is capable of responding to a perceived threat, and I know (in addition) the comparative threat levels they have assigned to the various positions in all this. Consider this carefully.

As some know, I have discontinued identifying myself as an advocate of the Federal Vision.[5]

Prior to making that disclaimer, I used to describe the Federal Vision advocates in terms of different kinds of beer. I was an FV amber ale, and Jim Jordan was an oatmeal stout. I considered my amber ale to be a version of classic Westminsterian theology, and the other end of the FV spectrum was an amalgam, as critics saw it, of Reformed theology, Biblical Horizons, Lutheranism, Anglicanism, and some deep weird. I am not saying this in a pejorative way—my point is elsewhere. So the most *outré* enemy for the PCA during that tumultuous time was, taking

---

5. I explain all of that here: https://dougwils.com/the-church/s16-theology/federal-vision-no-mas.html.

their take, an odd form of Lutheranism, and the denomination went absolutely bonkers over it. I mean, the place looked like the floor of the orangutan cages after a bout of diarrhea swept through the zoo. There were no mills of the gods grinding away, exceedingly fine. No, there was yelling, and shouting, and pushing, and blogging, and books, and yelling, and resolutioning, and charges brought, and anathematizing, and more blogging, and names called and names named.

The courts of the PCA were certainly involved—but they were involved *because of* the larger controversy. The ministers of the PCA cared about the issue, and *acted* like they cared about the issue, and acted in *public* like they cared about the issue.

I am not here addressing whether they got all the issues right or wrong. I am simply observing—*as someone who knows first-hand*—that the PCA knows how to react if they think someone is trying to bring something from outside, Canterbury or Wittenberg say, to their Geneva. Assuming a perceived threat, they know how to do it.

So, how do you think they responded when someone proposed bringing queer treasure into the New Jerusalem? How do you think they responded when a PCA church sponsored a conference using all the LGBTQ+ jargon? Don't you love that *plus*? What's under *that*, I wonder? Actually, nobody wonders. We all *know* what's under there. How do you think they responded when Covenant Seminary cozied up to the event, keeping *just* the right distance, thus demonstrating their expertise in plausible deniability?

Stop. You're making me yawn.

Where Did All the Valiant-for-Truths Go?

The last time I came through these parts, there were thousands of men, Tarzan-like, beating their chests and crying out, *solasolasolafeeeeedei.* Where'd they all go? I have married a wife, I have bought me a cow.

I am going to put this as bluntly as I can. The threat facing the PCA over the sexual revolution, and all its attendant issues, is many times greater than the threat posed by the Federal Vision. This would even be the case even if everything that all the critics said about the Federal Vision were true, and were true clean through.

Ponder this. The threat of the sexual revolution, the sexual tsunami that is about to hit the PCA beaches, is a gargantuan threat, and there has been virtually no response to speak of. The wake caused by the FV speedboat sloshed over their feet, and carried somebody's flip flop out into the river, and the whole denomination came unstuck.

Why No Response?

The Revoice conference was a vanguard move. It was an incursion into the world of the PCA to find out how hard—or soft as the case may be—the defenses were. Behind those initial forays by technically-celibate Christiany speakers are the massed armies of the secular world

Why no fight? Why no valor? I am reminded of the definition of valor in Ambrose Bierce's *Devil's Dictionary.* "

> VALOR, n. A soldierly compound of vanity, duty and the gambler's hope.
>
> "Why have you halted?" roared the commander of a division at Chickamauga, who had ordered a charge; "move forward, sir, at once."
>
> "General," said the commander of the delinquent brigade, "I am persuaded that any further display of valor by my troops will bring them into collision with the enemy."

Declaring war on the Federal Vision got you some inside-baseball orthodoxy points, and was a good career move within the denomination. But declaring war on the sexual revolution might get you in some real trouble. It might cost you something substantial, out in the real world. You see, that handful of Revoice presenters represented what most *think* will be the future of the country, and therefore the PCA, and what not a few *want* to be the future of the PCA, and the country.

Cowards on the ramparts. Cowards in the citadels. Cowards in the corridors. Cowards in the seminaries. Cowards in the publishing houses. Cowards at the conferences. Cowards on the sessions. Cowards in the presbyteries. Cowards in the pulpit. A sea of frothing pink cowardice.

I know basic ecclesiastical physics. I know where your rock is, and I know where they have placed the fulcrum. I know how long and how sturdy their lever is. I can see what they are doing, and it doesn't matter how many individual people you know who "disagree" with it. When the mainline Presbyterians lost their denomination, about eighty percent of their ministers were still orthodox and evangelical. They also didn't know where the fulcrum was, and where the lever was.

"Doctor, how is it possible for him to have died? I can't believe it. Most of his body *didn't* have cancer . . ."

To all this, the technically and ostensibly orthodox will want to wail: "But the situation is so complicated, and seems so hopeless. We don't know what to doooooo . . ."

"I'll tell you what. Why don't you pretend that, instead of saying that we should 'bring queer treasure into the New Jerusalem,' the presenters at Revoice had said something really bad, something that sounded like Norman Shepherd, something like 'justifying faith working through love.' Take it from there. Start throwing things."

So here it is. If you are in the PCA, barring a miracle from Heaven, your denomination is finished. You demonstrated first in the FV brawl that you knew how to fight, and are demonstrating now, when the threat is orders of magnitude greater, that you can't be bothered. There is therefore no excuse.

In Conclusion, Let Me Make Myself a Litmus Test

Unless and until your leaders stop caring what all the respectable people think about Wilson, and start caring, a whole lot more, about what Wilson thinks about all the respectable people, your church is deceased. Departed. Toast. Finis. Caput. Bought the farm. Done. Handed in its lunch bucket.

"Yeah, well, we would have been willing to listen to some of your insights if you had not gone off on that Southern slavery jag. *You're* the one who wrecked it."

"The fight about Southern slavery was not an apologetic for slavery at all. It was an apologetic for the plain teaching of the *Bible*. And we were fighting that fight, decades ago, back in the nineties, because we saw *where* they were placing the fulcrum, and what lever they were going to use. We saw what sexual direction the rock was going to flip. And everything is unfolding just as we predicted. You should have listened then also."

Either believe the Bible, *all* of it, or just cut to the chase and call yourself a liberal. And once you are a liberal, there will be absolutely no remaining principle of resistance when the LGBTQ plussers are speaking confidently at the microphones of *your* General Assemblies.

So whatever you say, apart from massive repentance, your beloved denomination is going to assume room temperature shortly. Count on it.

There is a good bit more to say about all of this, but I think this
is sufficient for now.

CHAPTER SIX

Those BioLogos Unbelievers

Eugene Genovese once wrote that, during his atheist days, whenever he was in the company of a liberal Christian, he always felt that comfortable sense that he was in the presence of a fellow unbeliever. Unbelief is a thing.

And that matter of faith is always the basic issue. One of the New Testament names for Christians is the simple term *believers* (Acts 5:14; 1 Tim. 4:12). When Jesus would admonish His disciples, one of the ways He would do it was through His stinging phrase "ye of little faith" (Matt. 6:30; 8:26; 14:31).

The Westminster Confession is full of pastoral wisdom, and does know that saving with can be "different in degrees, weak or strong" and "may often and many ways [be] assailed, and weakened" (14.3). But at the same time they do *not* allow the frailties and foibles of various Christians to be the determining factor in *defining* the essence of what saving faith is always called to do. "By this faith, a Christian *believes to be true whatsoever is revealed in the Word*" (14.2; emphasis added).

This would have to include Genesis. Saving faith believes to be true *whatsoever* is revealed in the Word. Mull that over.

And Genesis was not composed of some gumby-like material, and is not a text that can be shaped into whatever form is currently needed to maintain respectability out there in the world. Someone who can read Genesis and find millions of years in there, not to mention those years occupied with turning crickets into condors, is someone who could be appointed to the Supreme Court, open his copy of the Constitution, and discover in it that we are supposed to have three senators from every state.

Believers are supposed to, you know, believe things. And they are supposed to believe *what was written*. So when it comes to the first eleven chapters of Genesis, when someone in the Church tells us they "don't believe that it means . . ." our response should be, "Exactly so. And that's the problem. Not a small one either."

Cancer doesn't arrive all at once, pervading the body in ten minutes. The cancer of unbelief will take root in one place, and then spread to the others. Too often our debates about theological liberalism (just a fancy name for this unbelief) are over whether the patient has *died* yet, when they ought to be over whether the patient has cancer yet. There is a type of naïve observer who will accept that a denomination is going liberal after it has died of that liberalism. They will only accept a diagnosis of liberalism from the coroner, never from the doctors. So prior to that point where the farm is actually purchased, when something could still be done about it, denial is the name of the game. And so it is—*anyone* who admits any kind of funny business into Genesis 1-11, while they may not be dead in their liberalism, they do have a case of it.

The evangelical church today is shot through with this spirit of unbelief; we are riddled with cancer. We flat *don't* believe "whatsoever is revealed." It perhaps began with a few in the pews who have trouble with this or that. Then it spreads to men who are great when it comes to the New Testament, or with systematic theology generally considered, but who function with a quiet unbelief running in the background when it comes to things like theistic evolution. There have been more than a few evangelical worthies who have made their quiet peace with this kind of evolution, adopting some theistic form of it—men like John Stott, or J.I. Packer. But because the devil is a zealous evangelist, it then proceeds to an active and energetic advocacy of that unbelief, such as what we see from N.T. Wright, or James K.A. Smith. This is the BioLogos approach. If you go to the BioLogos website, the first thing you will see is a picture of Tim Keller there.[6] Keller is one of the stars in the PCA firmament, and this is yet one more reason the PCA is in big trouble. If you are shopping for a house, you don't buy one with a crumbling foundation. The doctrine of creation is *foundational*, and theistic evolution provides nothing but the crumble. Bad combination.

Now Keller thinks he is calling non-Christians to an acceptable faith, but he is actually calling Christians to an acceptable unbelief.[7]

---

6. This was the case at the time of writing, but is not the case now. So don't go check. Save your breath for walking uphill.

7. If you are interested, an earlier take of mine on BioLogos can be found here—https://dougwils.com/books-and-culture/s7-engaging-the-culture/7-reasons-why-biologos-is-a-threat-to-classical-christian-education.html—and here—https://dougwils.com/books-and-culture/s21-atheism-and-apologetics/does-tim-keller-live-on-an-old-earth.html.

You Science Denier, You

We have been told, multiple times we have been told, that we cannot possibly hold to something like young-earth creationism, and also win the respect of mainstream scientists.

You know, there was a time in my callow youth when I might have at least felt the force of this argument. Wouldn't have agreed with it, wouldn't have gone along with it, but I at least had the modesty to *feel* like a goober for thinking God made the earth 6,000 years ago. I mean, look at all those scientists, guys with fifty pound heads, lined up in their white lab coats, and with framed copies of all their Nobel Prizes hanging on the wall in the background. But that was back in the days before respectable science went barking mad, and started barging into furniture, rolling on the floor, and chewing on the edges of the carpet. We now live in times in which I confess that I am not interested at all in winning the respect of mainstream science. Winning that respect would be a real danger sign.

Take this as my version of my back pages. I was so much older then; I'm younger than that now. Just by remaining right where I was, simply by not budging, my science-denying has just simply taken wings. What does my science-denying now include? I am not freaked out by minor changes in the weather, and do not believe "climate change" can be invoked to justify every passing Democratic policy proposal that involves spending buckets of money, which would be all of them. My science-denying thinks that sunspots might have more to do with fluctuations in the weather than does letting my truck idle long in the winter to warm up.

My science-denial now includes thinking that boys are chromosomally boys, and shall remain such, and that the same thing goes for girls. I know, right? Next stop: flat earthery! I also have the hubris to take issue with the nation's certified pediatricians (as though *I* knew anything about medicine!), differing with their view that pre-pubescent boys and girls should be allowed to go under the knife to remove perfectly healthy sexual organs. And for my crowning shame, I am one of the nation's scientific troglodytes, one who believes that all women have vaginas.

Look. If people want the science-denial argument to work anymore—which it incidentally doesn't—they need to factor in the effect that the red clown nose of political correctness, and the Groucho glasses of trendy leftism, are having on the general public. They kind of wipe out the moral authority of the white lab coat. They need to start factoring in how obvious it is to everyone that intellectual fads and moral panics determine what sort of scientific results are publishable.

God of the Gaps

Evolutionists are fond of accusing creationists of appealing to the "God of the gaps," hauling God in—the ultimate *Deus ex machina*—in order to make our risible views about origins "work" somehow. Let's take a moment to deal with this because it reveals a category mistake on their part—and it is not a small one.

Creationists are thorough-going supernaturalists. The simple fact of *creatio ex nihilo* is a grand miracle. The active presence of God in a fundamentally miraculous enterprise, like creation from nothing, is no problem at all. It is what we are *arguing* for. But if someone has a naturalistic system that gets into trouble periodically, and the supernatural is brought in to resolve the insoluble problem, see accompanying cartoon, then that actually is a problem.[8] And take a good look at that car-

---

8. The cartoon features two professors looking at a blackboard with complicated equations with "THEN A MIRACLE OCCURS" in the middle, to which one professor replies, "I think you should be more explicit here in step two."

toon, because theistic evolution requires a chain of events just like that, with over a hundred billion links in it. And then *another* miracle occurs!

We have already demonstrated how silly naturalistic evolution is. Now what do we call it when God is brought in to save such a teetery system?

So a "God of the gaps" problem *does* occur when you bring in some supernatural power to make something work that you don't really understand. But creationists are appealing to God to accomplish something remarkable because we *do* understand it. What we understand is that iPhones don't assemble themselves, and so if one shows up in my pocket, then we conclude that somebody else *made* it and *sold* it to me. So if all we are doing is simply maintaining that Apple makes iPhones, we would certainly be left unimpressed if somebody accused us of holding to a "corporation of the gaps" approach. Quite. Our thesis is that *made* things are *made* by somebody. That's the whole *point* we are making.

So for strict creationists, the nothing out of which God created everything is the ultimate gap, and so we simply believe in *God*, not God joining forces with nothing, as though nothing were some pre-existing material. Or, if you must, we affirm the God of the gap, *singular*. To affirm the God of the gap, singular, is simply to affirm the Creator/creature distinction. He spoke, and it was.

But naturalistic evolution presents us with the ultimate and unworkable contraption, Rube Goldberging its way down through the millennia, staggering along, with an unbridgeable gap happening, naturalistically speaking, every ten minutes or so. When all those gaps are crossed because God intervened in the process—*that* really is a "God of the gaps." That really is special pleading.

So theistic evolutionists really are appealing to the "God of the gaps"—not in order to make creation a reasonable thing, but to make evolution even possible. And that, incidentally, is the only way to make it possible. If God can make sons of Abraham out of rocks, then He certainly could make a sperm whale out of cow. Sure. Whether He did or not is a separate question, but the person who postulates a long chain of such events is the one guilty of all the special pleading. Theistic evolutionists are the ones who worship the "God of the gaps." Creationists do not.

Real Evangelism Doesn't Compromise

Compromised evangelism tries to figure out a way to make Christianity attractive to non-Christians. Real evangelism seeks a way—already knowing that the only way to do this is through preaching the cross—to make rebellious non-Christians acceptable to God, and to the faith once delivered. Sinners need to be modified in order be fitted into the Church. The Church does *not* need to be modified in order to make sure sinners feel comfy when they come. Unbelievers within the Church feel like the church has something to prove to the infidel—proving against all hope that the Church is somehow worthy of their patronage. But believers within the Church, true sons and daughters of the Church, believe that the repentant infidel is the one who has to bear fruits worthy of repentance.

And as the anti-Darwinist[9] C.S. Lewis points out somewhere, the accommodationist edges of a compromised faith are not usually where radical non-believers come when they are converted. When a queer theorist lesbian academic like Rosaria Butterfield is converted, it is not into the soft feminism of quasi-complemen-tarianism. When the fire-eating atheist is converted, it is not to a liberal Unitarianism. No, when outsiders come in, they come all

9. See Jerry Bergman, *C.S. Lewis Anti-Darwinist.*

the way *in*. If they repent of their unbelief, they are not attracted
to the Christianized veneer forms of that same spirit of unbelief.

BioLogos Is Allergic to the Text of Scripture

As the rot of unbelief works its way through the content of what
some folks are willing to affirm, one particular staging area for their
future forays into deeper unbelief is the affirmation that they are
"red letter" Christians. They build the hopes of their future apos-
tasies on the firm foundation of the very words of Jesus. They are
Jesus-followers—that pestilent fellow Paul irritates them, and Moses
makes them feel icky all over.

Now it would be more to the point to say that they are in love with
the *idea* of being red-letter Christians, but this can only be pulled off
if they refuse to examine too closely what the Lord Jesus actually said.
I say this because a bunch of the red letters talk about the black letters.

As the joke goes—I have a special edition of the Bible, where all
the words of the Holy Spirit are in black.

What did Jesus think about the black letters? "If he called them
gods, unto whom the word of God came, *and the scripture cannot be
broken*" (Jn. 10:35; emphasis added).

What did Jesus think about the historicity of the first eleven
chapters of Genesis? Well, for starters, He based His teaching on divorce on the fact of it. "And he answered and said unto them, Have
ye not read, that *he which made them at the beginning* made them male
and female," (Matt. 19:4; emphasis added).

What did Jesus assume about the historicity of the fourth human
being to walk on this earth? "That upon you may come all the righteous blood shed upon the earth, *from the blood of righteous Abel* unto

the blood of Zacharias son of Barachias, whom ye slew between the temple and the altar" (Matt. 23:35; emphasis added).

And what did Jesus think about that really embarrassing part of Genesis 1-11? You know, the (*ho, ho, ho*) worldwide Flood? "For as in the days that were before the flood they were eating and drinking, marrying and giving in marriage, *until the day that Noe entered into the ark*" (Matt. 24:38; emphasis added).

One response to all this is to say that Jesus was simply stepping into the customs and assumptions of His day, or perhaps He was simply making literary allusions—you know, the way an English teacher might say "as Tom Sawyer said." The defect in this approach is that they are trying to make out that Jesus was as much of an unbeliever as they are. "Whosoever therefore shall be ashamed of me *and of my words* in this adulterous and sinful generation; of him also shall the Son of man be ashamed, when he cometh in the glory of his Father with the holy angels" (Mark 8:38; emphasis added).

So if your forehead gets hot when you look at what Jesus actually said about Adam and Eve, and Abel, and Noah, then you need to run a serious spiritual inventory, and admit to yourself that you are ashamed of His words. The next step is to recognize that He will be ashamed of you at His coming, and that presents a higher level of difficulty, at least for you.

If you don't want to believe, then I would invite you to go find another religion to degrade. There were purported miracles surrounding the Buddha. Why don't you go doubt them?

BioLogos Is in Love With Natural Evil

The great irony is that in their desire to answer the "what about science and evolution?" question, and to answer it by capitulating, the theistic evolutionists create a situation where the "what about natural evil and the goodness of God?" question becomes—given their framework—unanswerable.

It is no great apologetics strategy to surrender your rook, two knights, a bishop, and a queen, in order to take their pawn.

Why is there suffering? Why is there natural evil? Why is nature red in tooth and claw? Why is there bone cancer? Why are there earthquakes and volcanos and tornados? Why have so many millions of creatures with exquisitely tuned central nervous systems suffered such agonistic deaths over the millennia?

The answer can have nothing to do with the rebellion of man, for that rebellion happened—*if* it happened, note, because the unbelief is now eroding their belief in the Fall—at the very tail end of the many long ages of this suffering. So the reason for all the suffering must be that God looked down, smiled on it, and said, "behold, it is very good." God loves all that suffering, and if He does, then so must the theistic evolutionists love it.

The only alternative to this, the only way out, is to jettison even more of the faith. They must get rid of the *entire* doctrine of creation from nothing, and to opt for some form of panentheism—where God didn't actually *create* the mess, and is struggling with the simple fact of it, all outside His immediate control, just like the rest of us struggle with it. Our inadequate god would fix it if he could. More than a few of these johnnies are on the threshold of doing exactly this, and when they take that final step, the faithful will stand on the walls of the City of God, and look sadly upon their apostate departure. All we can see of them anymore are asses and elbows. They did leave behind a few scholarly articles.

Genesis: Love It or Leave It

The doctrine of creation is not something that a creature should simply be "okay" with. Let us kneel before the Lord our God our Maker. The doctrine of creation is our foundational *glory*. "In the beginning God created the heaven and the earth" (Gen. 1:1).

How did the entire cosmos get here? Someone just *said* it. "By the word of the LORD were the heavens made; And all the host of them by the breath of his mouth . . . For he spake, and it was done; He commanded, and it stood fast" (Ps. 33:9).

The stars showed up, just like that, and started singing. "Let them praise the name of the LORD: For he commanded, and they were created" (Ps. 148:5).

He didn't just slap it all together either. He crafted every atom in every star in all wisdom, and placed each one of them perfectly. "The LORD by wisdom hath founded the earth; By understanding hath he established the heavens" (Prov. 3:19).

He calls every star by name, and does so in a way that does not appear to cater to our spirit of unbelief. In fact, the biblical narrative tramples all over our spirit of unbelief. "Lift up your eyes on high, And behold who hath created these things, That bringeth out their host by number: He calleth them all by names By the greatness of his might, for that he is strong in power; Not one faileth" (Is. 40:26).

All His works are perfect. "And God saw every thing that he had made, and, behold, it was very good. And the evening and the morning were the sixth day" (Gen. 1:31).

And prior to the sin of man, Eden was, well, Edenic. Not an agonistic Botch Job, spanning millennia. It really was very good. And all the believers said, *amen and amen.*

CHAPTER SEVEN

Against Justice

The immediate question that may arise is "what kind of monster could be 'against justice?'" If this were not November, I would perhaps say that this is a reasonable question and proceed to answer it in my customary way, full to overflowing with balance and nuance. But that doesn't keep it from being, at bottom, a stupid question.

There are two kinds of justice that merit our strongest opposition. They are, respectively, justice-falsely-so-called, at any time, as we see with the social justice movement, but also real justice, biblically-defined, when someone is demanding it immediately.

Of course we should be able to instantly see why we wouldn't want false justice at any time. We don't want it for the same reason we don't want people in our store buying things with counterfeit twenty dollar bills. But why would we not want *real* justice instantly? The answer is that—barring the events surrounding the Second

Coming—if you get real justice instantly, it isn't real justice. Justice is corrupted, not only by means of radical SJW redefinition, but it is also redefined whenever it is bustled or hurried along by sinners.

Solutions and Trade-offs

The great Thomas Sowell put his finger on the essential difference between conservatives and progressives when he said, "There are no solutions; there are only trade-offs." Progressives always think in terms of solutions. They see a problem, and they want it fixed *instanter*. "What do we want?" *Justice!* "When do we want it?" *Now!* Conservatives know that everything costs something, so if we take a particular course of action, it too will cost something. Is that a cost we want to pay?

This is also the difference between a reformer and a revolutionary. A revolutionary is impatient, and in that impatience, he wrecks the world. An impatient reformer is therefore a revolutionary, regardless of what he calls himself. A real reformer knows that some of the social problems we are addressing will take two hundred years to fix. Consequently, he will not be easily elected in an impatient age. Fortunately, the reforms he has in mind are not brought about by elections, but by evangelism, church planting, more evangelism, discipleship, and missions.

The apostle Paul did not arrive in Rome with a sure-fire "plan" for eliminating the gladiatorial games. He arrived with a gospel that did in fact eliminate them, but it took centuries.

A progressive on the campaign trail is someone who promises *solutions*—"real solutions for the hard-working American people." A conservative is someone who knows that whatever you decide to do, there will be real costs associated with it. Sometimes those costs are worth paying, but most of the time they are not. They are especially not worth paying when no one involved in the decision-making paid the slightest bit of attention to them throughout the course of the debate. They are almost always *enormous* costs when they have been assiduously hidden by those who have a lust for power.

We can see how foolish this progressivist-lust-cycle is when we consider that the thing requiring "solutions" in this particular campaign is actually the bundle of problems caused by the *last* round of "solutions." Whenever simple solutions are imposed, there will come a time when the bills come due. And when the bills come due, some politician is going to arise, demanding solutions to the pressing problem of these "bills" that are mysteriously "due." So he proposes a sweeping Reform Bill. What problems will it solve? It will solve all the problems created by the *last* Reform Bill, the one proposed by the previous senator from the great state of Minnesostastan.

Patience Is Hard

One of the things I periodically say in the course of pastoral counseling is something like this: "Remember that there is no problem so bad but that you cannot make it worse." But I try to say it encouragingly, and with a smile.

If this is true in the lives of individuals, and in marriages and in families, *as it most certainly is*, then how much more is it the case when we are talking about societies with millions of people in them? What are the ways in which we might make things worse? How might all this go wrong? Conservatives ask these sorts of questions, and progressives do not. And when conservatives *stop* asking them, this is the surest indicator that they have begun the long march leftward.

Pick a social problem, any social problem, from any point in history. A caravan moving toward the southern border. All-white restaurants refusing service to blacks. Widespread groping in the movie industry. Gladiatorial games in honor of Vespasian. Inheritance laws that require everything going to the firstborn son. Communist spies throughout the State Department in the 1950s. Abortion on demand in post-*Roe* America.

Now here's the problem. I want you to craft a "solution" to any one of those problems, and I want you to do so with the proviso that ten years after your solution is implemented, whatever mechanism you came up with will be taken over and used by the enemies of God.

The American Founders devised just such a system. They wanted a form of government that they would be willing to live under if their worst enemies won the next three elections in a row.

This is nothing other than the Golden Rule applied to practical politics. Give the CIA precisely the amount of power you would want them to have if Hillary Clinton had won the election.

Is that one too easy? Okay, so let's make you a hard one.

Say we are confronted with a problem of racist B&Bs. Such Bed and Breakfast joints reserve the right to refuse service to anyone which, in this hypothetical situation, would mean anyone with darker skin than theirs. Okay, that's your problem. Now I want you to craft legislation that deals with such discrimination, and do so with the knowledge that ten years after the passage of your legislation, the machinery you have created (if indeed you were foolish enough to create some) will be taken over by the homosexual lobby.

So am I saying that the Civil Rights Act of 1964 was not thought through carefully? That is exactly what I am saying. The fact that you have the moral high ground when it comes to all the intended

consequences does not protect you in the slightest from all the un-
foreseen unintended consequences. And—incidentally—your facile
ability to accuse me of racism because I care about unintended consequences is one of the more egregious unintended consequences.

Leftward, Ho

We are living in a time when multiple evangelical organizations—denominations, publishers, parachurch organizations, etc.—are steadi-
ly moving left. Hardly any are moving in a genuinely conservative
direction. In some cases the problem is open and flagrant, while in
others it is simply a worrisome possibility.

But regardless of who you are worried about—the SBC, the
PCA, American Vision, InterVarsity, the Gospel Coalition, you
name it—do not settle for fig leaf affirmations, as though that
settles anything. "They still have inerrancy in their statement of
faith." And don't look for whether they believe in "cultural engagement." Cultural engagement is frequently the code mantra that
is being chanted in the course of cultural surrender. Real cultural
engagement is conservative, slow, reformational. Spurious cultural
engagement is hot and impatient.

So listen for them echoing the world's refrain. Take note of that
spirit of impatience—particularly impatience with conservatives.
Whenever someone wants to read the fine print, when someone
wants to examine the price tag and gets out his calculator and everybody starts yelling at him *and* his racist math, you have identified
the problem.

So regardless of what they say, it is not possible for sound
Christians to believe in "solutions."

CHAPTER EIGHT

Immodest Wenches

My point in this post is not—lest someone mistake my point—to do anything so simple as decry immodest attire in women. And by the kind of *immodesty* I am not for the most part talking about, I am intending both definitions of that word—viz. that which is sexual provocative, and that which is flamboyant and ostentatious. Get that? The kind of immodesty that is not my principal point is both kinds of immodesty. Like I say, this point is somewhat more complicated than that. Have I lost you already?

Now in saying that this is *not* my objective, it is not to say such a task would be an unworthy objective. No, it would be absolutely fine, as the occasion calls for it, and great writers have, before now, poured their considerable talents into the task.

> Moreover the LORD saith, Because the daughters of Zion
> are haughty, and walk with stretched forth necks and wanton
> eyes, walking and mincing as they go, and making a tinkling
> with their feet: Therefore the Lord will smite with a scab the
> crown of the head of the daughters of Zion, and the LORD
> will discover their secret parts. (Isa. 3:16–17)

The daughters of Zion were apparently strutting their stuff down 5th Avenue, and the prophet Isaiah apparently took note of it. And this has been a problem in other eras as well. Consider the pithy observations of Nathaniel Ward, an observer of Puritan New England back in the 17th century.

> I honor the woman that can honor herself with her attire . . .
> a good text always deserves a fair margin, but as for a woman
> who lives but to ape the newest court-fashions, I look at her as
> the very gizzard of a trifle, the product of a quarter of cipher,
> the epitome of nothing; fitter to be kicked, if she were of a
> kickable substance, than either honored or humored . . . It is no
> marvel they wear trails on the hinder part of their heads; hav-
> ing nothing it seems in the forepart but a few squirrels' brains
> to help them frisk from one ill-favored fashion to another.[10]

This is the kind of observation that today will get you labeled a misogynist. "Look, he attacked all women in a vicious and unprovoked way!" Well, actually, he divided women into two groups, the honorable ones and the silly ones, and he critiqued the silly ones.

10 Nathaniel Ward, *On the Frivolities of Fashion*, in Edmund Stedman and Ellen Hutchinson eds., *A Library of American Literature: An Anthology in Eleven Volumes* (New York: Charles Webster, 1892), 1:276.

"But an attack on silly women is, in our book, an attack on all women!" *Ummm* . . .

I will leave it to the logic students among us to figure out who the misogynists are, and press on to my real point.

Our Fun House

As cultures wax and wane, as societies rise and fall, as civilizations emerge from their hardscrabble pioneering days only to throw all their hard-won virtue into a vat of *fin de siècle* goo, we have always had certain times when the women were bundled up appropriately, and then we have had other times when they were liberated from the constraints of both customs and corsets. That, as I say, is nothing new. Societies do alternate between decent and indecent. England in the 18th century was indecent, and by the Victorian era a century later, they were all buttoned up tight.

We have had times when the men were voyeurs and the women exhibitionists. We have had other times when the women were modest and the men sought to respect that. This is our unusual fun house time—a time when women are exhibitionists and the men are required to pretend they are nothing of the kind.

G.K. Chesterton once said that our problem was not that we lived in a skeptical age. Our problem was that we lived in a dogmatic age without knowing it. The schizophrenic delusion that provoked Chesterton's jibe is the same delusion that has convinced our generation that we are sexual liberated, when we are actually prudish.

This is another way of saying we live in a time when all of us, particularly the remaining normal folks, are being gas lit. Provocations abound, and if you notice them, or say anything about them, it will be taken as sure evidence that *you* are the one losing your mind. If you say anything about how licentious the orgy has become, you will be shushed as though everybody is sitting around in the library, clothed and in their right mind.

So as the sexual revolution works its way into its Robespierre/guillotine stages, we are getting to the point where everybody is simultaneously licentious *and* prudish. An actress can go to a party where she has slept with half the men in the room, and if someone there makes an unwanted suggestive remark, a blush comes to her maidenly cheek, and she draws herself to her full height, and tosses her curls. She can then give an interview to an investigative reporter, agog at the Babylonian excesses being related, and she can describe how her producer had asked her up to his room in order to discuss the story arc of their current project, and had then come on to her, and how she had had simply *no idea*. Never mind that she has *in her contract*, a document that *she* signed, her agreement to take off all her clothes for the camera if that same man had deemed it necessary in the cause of Art.

Art is a guy in the casting office, a lecher on the creepier end of things.

If this were not November, this would be the place where a nuanced and most sensible qualification would have its very own paragraph. True to my word, I leave it entirely out. All the reasonable readers can guess what it would have been, and all the unreasonable readers would ignore it anyway.

Demanding a Cloak of Invisibility for Public Sin Is Not the Same Thing as Privacy

A number of years ago, a married couple who worked for some institution—I think it was a hospital—did their own home-made porno flick, which they then posted online. This was discovered by someone, and both of them were fired. Thereupon they turned around and sued the hospital *for invading their privacy*.

Like a toddler hiding from everybody in the family by sitting in the middle of the living room floor and covering his eyes, there is a failure here to grasp the concept. And here is the concept—what is done in public *can be seen*.

Suppose there is some church function or other, and one of the edgy church ladies wears something, or almost wears something, that is kind of outrageous. Too short, too tight, too loose—there are many options here, filling out additional meaning for the *too* in #MeToo. Everybody in the room now knows more about her breasts than any of them were supposed to know. When she was dressing for the event, she was not exactly mulling over 1 Timothy 2:9—her most recent Bible memory verse . . . "likewise also that women should adorn themselves in respectable apparel, with modesty and self-control . . . ."

No, that wasn't exactly on her mind. What *was* on her mind was tweaking the Puritans. Showing that "edgy church lady" is not oxymoronic. Demonstrating that some free spirits have not been stifled with all that Pauline theology. Declaring to the world that she is marching to a different drummer.

Now remember my point. It is not that one of the Puritans might eventually be provoked into saying something. Sure, that might happen. But the point is that if a normal person ever did say something about the unnecessary display . . . *that* is the point where the *provocatrice* would turn into one of our new kind of Puritan, hauling into the discussion a tangled web of scruples, rules, prohibitions, compunctions, anxieties, and offenses.

And the person with the problem is the one who notices the problem. The whole thing is more than a little bit convenient.

Don't Forget the Squirrel Brains

One other category needs to be mentioned, but just briefly. There are any number of sweet Christian girls who dress in the inappropriate way they do because their roommates and sisters lie to them routinely ("that's *so* cute . . ."). They are just being clueless, although it should be granted they are being more clueless than they have a right to be. But at the same time they are being clueless in a new world that has been shaped by the *provocatrices* and the lechers who underwrite them. Being cute little squirrels, they don't get the larger picture. So if someone did take them aside to give a little friendly admonition, they would be humiliated down into the ground. They would be devastated. There would be many tears. They might have to go into counseling.

But the real discipline would land elsewhere. In the meantime, the person who spoke to them about it would be run out of town as a rape apologist.

All is proceeding as planned.

CHAPTER NINE

Sexual Imbecility for Imbeciles

The prodigal son didn't run out of money his first week away from home. He was able to afford the best beer, the best women, the best time for all concerned, and to do so for a goodly amount of time. The wisdom of his plan was not falsified by events at the *front* end of his bender.

If someone, in the grip of a sheer delusion, jumped off one of those bridges where people do their bungee-jumping, and did so without being attached to *anything*, the sensations he would experience for a few ecstatic moments would be indistinguishable from the sensations of flying. He would *feel* like he was flying. The wind would blow through his hair *like* he was flying. The ground might be starting to look ominous, and it might appear that he is flying mostly downwards. But still he was flying.

Feelings reign supreme around here, and so it feels like flying. But there is a narrative arc for all our creaturely stories, and so there will come that inevitable moment when it feels more like—culling some wisdom from one of those online lists of bad metaphors—hitting the rocks below "like a Hefty bag filled with vegetable soup." Not at all like flying.

The Predictive Power of Premises

We need not inquire too closely into the outcome of the delusional behavior. It will end as all such delusions do—either in the nut house or in the morgue. What we actually want to do in the meantime is protect any of our loved ones from getting swept up into the lunacy. We want to protect our children and our friends and neighbors. We want to protect all our fellow church members from buying into the general asininity. Most of all, we need to prevent the Big Names of Evangelicalism from going woke-gonzo. Let me tell you, there is nothing worse than seeing squishy evangelicals with a platform going woke-gonzo.

But we cannot do this simply by predicting our dire Hefty bag outcome. Those in the grip of the delusion have been forearmed against all our warnings. Have they not seen *all* the sitcoms where the crazy crotchety uncle offered some throwback sentiment about the loveable and obligatory homo-character, and have they not heard for themselves how that poor man was hooted back to his Neanderthal cave by the laugh track? If that's not refutation, I don't know what is.

So you are talking to someone up on the bungee-jumping bridge, and you know that they are starting to think about it. He has already dismissed your dire prediction—something about "getting killed"—for, he says, reasoning closely, "In my Superman mode, I can fly." Perhaps it might be more effective to tackle that premise. His Superman mode is not a thing.

For your friend, teetering on the edge of sanity, is still reasoning validly. His conclusions would follow, granting the premises. But why on earth did we ever grant the premises? A valid argument will always have a true conclusion, provided the premises are true. But whether the premises are true is a question of fact. Not only that, but the diabolical forces in charge of all this know exactly what they are doing, and so they guard those premises with a massive wall of erudite scorn. You will see what I mean in moment when I get to those premises, and sketch them out for you.

The problem is that for at least half a century now, Christians have been granting the false premises of secularism, and then trying to dispute with them over perfectly valid chains of thought. It is not working. How could it work? Granting their premises, what they are doing is perfectly reasonable. And since their conclusion are insane, and they are reasoning validly, that must mean the insanity is embedded in the premises.

Two Sets of Premises

The Christian view of society is built on this bedrock assumption: *God created the world, and we therefore must live under His law and authority.* The countervailing assumption coming from the secularists is this: *Space, time, and matter are the only ultimate reality, and so any form of matter can be transformed into any other configuration of matter.*

When God created the world, He did it by distinguishing this from that. He consistently, all the way through, puts this over here and that over there. God likes setting boundaries. He establishes dividing lines. He did this with heaven over here and earth over there (Gen. 1:1). He did it by placing the evening in this spot and the morning in that spot (Gen. 1:5). He rejoiced when He had the opportunity to place the land in one place and the sea in a complete-ly different place (Gen. 1:9). He made the sun to rule the day, and the moon to rule the night (Gen. 1:16). And at the very crown of this entire glorious process, He created man in His own image, male and female created He them (Gen. 1:27). Men are this way, and women are that way.

So earth cannot decide to go through reassignment surgery in order to become heaven. The land cannot start identifying as wet and soggy in order to become the sea. The sun cannot dim its light and go slumming as the moon. The morning and evening cannot swap clothes and go off pretending to be one another. And so also, a man pretending to be a woman is actually just a pretend-woman. A woman pretending to be a man is actually just a pretend-man.

So in the Christian framework, when God assigns us our spot, that is what theologians like to call "our spot."

But in the secularist framework, there is no need for God. Billions of years ago there was this pinprick singularity thing, not quite noth-ing, but almost nothing, but somehow having infinite density. Our best science to date has determined that one day a delinquent Who down in this particular Whoville, a kid named Morris with a bad acne problem and a troubled home life, set off a small explosive device (McClintok/Finch 2013). This was most probably an M-80, but Wiesenheimer disputes it (2015). Anyhow, all orthodox scientists are agreed that this set off a chain reaction, *blammo*, and space itself ballooned up to its current size. Given this indisputable account of our origins,[11] nothing could be plainer than the fact that absolutely anything goes in this cosmos. Anything can turn into anything else, and nobody can tell them different. And why shouldn't it be this way? If hyper-dense matter from the singularity can turn into crab

11. "Indisputable account" means that no orthodox scientists dispute it. And ortho-dox scientists are those who don't dispute things they oughtn't.

nebulae, and a field full of buttercups, *and* your drunk Uncle Walter, then turning a guy into a girl should be kind of child's play.

So if lipstick makes you feel pretty, Hank, then it is obviously time for a little bit of lipstick.

And This is Why . . .

If the material cosmos is infinitely malleable, and there is no God above us, then there is absolutely no reason why we may not tinker with our arrangements of atoms and eye shadow, genes and genitalia, boxers and panties. If we are just atoms banging our way down that great concourse of atoms, that great tale told by an idiot, full of sound and fury, signifying nothing, then of course Cole Porter nailed it. Anything goes.

Sex with robots. Sex with multiple partners. Female genital mutilation. Trannies in the restrooms at Target. Anal intercourse. Oral sex hook-up culture in junior high. No fault divorce. Fruitless marriages. Same sex mirage. Abortion carnage. An untouchable gay mafia in the Roman Catholic priesthood. The altar boys are, alas, not untouchable.

Our cultural car is careening down the other side of a very steep mountain, and we can't do a blessed thing about it because the brakes are out.

Evangelical Stockholm Syndrome

Our evangelical leaders and movers and shakers and hokey-pokiers have had the secularist gun pressed to their temples for so long that they have developed a kind of affinity with their captors. They have started to kind of see things their way. They have felt the heat and have started to see the light. There is apparently no intention whatever of being guilty of anything like faithful martyrdom.

For an example of the most recent ongoing capitulation consider the evangelical response to potential Sexual Orientation and Gender Identity (SOGI) legislation. The lame response by the National Association of Evangelicals (NAE) and the Council for Christian Colleges and Universities (CCCU) has been to try to work out an attempted truce. It is called Fairness for All, and it proposes to safeguard *both* religious liberty *and* LGBTQ+ rights.

I am reminded of Winston Churchill's definition of an appeaser as one who throws others to the crocodile in a bid to be the last one eaten.

Why is this kind of thing even a possibility? There are two basic reasons, the first practical and the second theological. The practical reason is that conservative donors have not yet caught on to the scam being run on them by ostensibly conservative colleges. The colleges will talk a big resistance game when hitting up the donors, while at the *same* time, behind closed doors they will be trying to cut a deal with the solons of Sodom. So keep your eyes on the actions of CCCU in the months to come. If they finalize their Fairness for All capitulation, their buckling, their surrender, their complete transformation into Craven & Crawling Colleges and Universities (CCCU), then donors should really move into their best "not one thin dime" mode.

Please take note: *The evangelical establishment has been almost completely overrun.*

The second reason is theological. Liars are not trustworthy. Any agreed upon truce that our appointed cowards work out for us will be a truce that will be violated at the first opportunity, as soon as it benefits them to violate it. Our putative leaders would have done better to remember Faithful's response to Adam the First in *The*

Pilgrim's Progress. "Then it came burning hot into my mind, whatever he said, and however he flattered, when he got me home to his House, he would sell me for a slave."

Religious liberty is a religious value. It is valued by Christians for deep theological reasons, and those reasons are not shared by the secularists *at all.* Any worldview that does not hesitate over dismembering millions of little babies will not hesitate to dismember their manifestly superficial agreement made with evangelicowards.

We cannot negotiate our way out of this. We cannot manage it. We cannot hire consultants to finesse it for us. Massaging the tumor is only going to stimulate blood flow and help it grow. The only way out is *repentance* and *deliverance.*

The only way out is repentance and deliverance.

Lest the point be missed, I would like to say that the only way out is repentance and deliverance.

But We Can't Even

I said above that in the Christian understanding of the world, we are created by God and are required to do as He says. This is true, but it is not the entire truth. That is the way created reality is, but there is another factor. We not only have the biblical premises that the first two chapters of Genesis give us, we also have to deal with the reality of the Fall that is outlined in the third chapter.

Put simply, the meaning of chapter three is that we all hate the meaning of the first two chapters.

This hatred of God and His ways is a necessary and inveterate habit with us, one that we cannot do anything about. Left to our own devices, therefore, we will necessarily spiral slowly toward our ultimate destination in the outer darkness. Anywhere where we will not have to deal with *Him*.

This is another way of saying that our natural condition is one of insanity. The end result of our pride and insolence is the same as it was for Nebuchadnezzar during his bovine sabbatical. Our sanity returns on the same basis and with the same understanding as when it returned to Nebuchadnezzar.

> And at the end of the days I Nebuchadnezzar lifted up mine eyes unto heaven, and mine understanding returned unto me, and I blessed the most High, and I praised and honoured him that liveth for ever, whose dominion is an everlasting dominion, and his kingdom is from generation to generation. (Dan. 4:34)

But this is not possible for us to do apart from an appeal to the death, burial, and resurrection of Jesus Christ. We are in desperate need of *gospel*, and this is the only gospel there is. Christ died for sinners, and we fit that bill. Christ died for moral imbeciles, and we qualify there also. Christ died for proud and insolent rebels, and once again it appears we might be in possession of the only basis for appealing to Him.

So put all this together, and you will see what America needs to do if America is to be saved. First, we have to confess that God is the Creator of heaven and earth, and we must deny Darwinism, root and branch. Second, we must therefore acknowledge that we are answerable to God and His law, which means denying our central lust, which is the lust for autonomy. And third, we have to confess the name of Jesus, and ask Him to take away our heart of stone, replacing it with a heart of flesh. We must do this because He died on the cross for the sins of moral imbeciles, just like us, and because He rose from the dead so that we need not return to that condition ever again.

No hope otherwise.

CHAPTER TEN

Modern Art and the Dearth of Culture

A number of decades ago, around the time of some of my first forays into public discussion (e.g., letters to the editor), I noticed that there were two topics that would cause other members of the general public to come unstuck in their responses. Those two topics were homosexuality and modern art.

It was hard not to notice a high level of defensiveness when it came to both topics. There seemed to be an inverse relationship between the defensiveness and the defensible.

One time, when the University of Idaho opened up an art gallery on our Main Street, using it to display the contributions of art students being trained in who-knows-what, I wrote a letter to the editor on that occasion. I said something like "the art gallery was a fine addition to our community, and that we should all be glad for it. And yet, most of the exhibits appeared to have been vandalized, and I wondered if anything could be done to beef up security."

There was a response from one gent, and I paraphrase, but it was something like *&^*%*ofritzinonthejimjam!*

Already Assumed

In order to understand what has happened to the world of the arts, in the realm of aesthetics, we have to understand something about human beings, and this is a characteristic not necessarily related to art. Here it is. Whenever any task is challenging and difficult, it is much easier to cop a pose than it is to rise to the challenge of whatever that tough thing is. Buying a Stetson is easier than driving the cattle to Abilene.

This is obviously behavior that deserves to be laughed at, and so— the best defense being a good offense—it is a behavior that has fine-tuned the art of scoffing in preemptive return. And therein lies a tale.

Biblical Christians know that we are not supposed to sit in the seat of scoffers, but we sometimes ignore how scoffing actually works. It is not scoffing to notice that something is objectively risible, and laugh accordingly. Scoffing occurs when it is simply assumed, *without any argument*, that something is dated, or passé, or clichéd, or hackneyed, or predictable—and all these words plus a few more are used—and a posture of superiority is simply assumed.

C.S. Lewis describes, using the example of flippancy, how this process works in his wonderful book *The Screwtape Letters*:

> But flippancy is the best of all. In the first place it is very economical. Only a clever human can make a real Joke about virtue, or indeed about anything else; any of them can be trained to talk as if virtue were funny. Among flippant people the Joke is always assumed to have been made. No one actually makes it; but every serious subject is discussed in a

manner which implies that they have already found a ridiculous side to it. If prolonged, the habit of Flippancy builds up around a man the finest armour plating against the Enemy that I know, and it is quite free from the dangers inherent in the other sources of laughter. It is a thousand miles away from joy; it deadens, instead of sharpening, the intellect; and it excites no affection between those who practise it.[12]

What I am talking about here is actually the very same process, only the thing that is assumed to have been done (when it hasn't been) is the arduous work of aesthetic theology, the practical disciplines of training and applying talent, and the related work of the critic, analyzing what has been done—all within the framework of a biblical worldview. All of this work is sneeringly assumed to have been done already, when it hasn't been at all, and the coterie of critics arising from the self-appointed guild of aesthetes, heaps scorn on the Philistine *bourgeoisie*. But the real Philistines are actually elsewhere. They are the ones running this scam.

It is the quiet assumption of aesthetic superiority without ever having to demonstrate any superiority whatever. After many decades of policing this all with a sneer, we have gotten to the point where the works of art are demonstrably inferior, and yet they continue to get away with this scam.

I said just above that a biblical worldview is necessary to this process. It is necessary in order to keep the whole endeavor from floating off into the fog of relativism. When there are no standards for any aspect of life, then how can there be any standards for this artistic aspect of life? Nothing remains—nothing that is, except for the sneer. The sneer becomes a permanent fixture.

---

12. *The Screwtape Letters* (1942; HarperOne, 2001), 56.

Two Ways

There are two ways for the artist, and one ends with the destruction of all artistry. There are two definitions of art, in other words.

One of them makes everything depend on the will of the artist. Art is defined as whatever an artist does. If an approved member of the guild produced it, then it is a work of art. Nothing determines what is or is not art but the intention of the artist.

And this is why the layman's critique—"my five-year-old could do better than that"—falls on deaf ears. That five-year-old, whatever his other merits, is not a member of the guild. The layman is appealing to a standard that was abandoned by the *illuminati* over a century ago.

The second definition of art, the Christian definition, requires a work of art to conform to an external and objective standard of beauty. That objective standard is grounded in the nature of God Himself—who is arrayed in the beauty of holiness—and when the artist reflects, captures, mirrors, reproduces, and holds something of that glory, the result is a work of art.

Does God Like It?

So the test for every aesthetic endeavor should be this: does God like it? The standard that every critic should apply is the same. Does God like it?

The immediate reaction to a statement like this among the soft evangelicals is to recoil, appalled. Does God like it? How are we supposed to know something like *that*? Are we supposed to assume that God wrote a book or something?

Yes, He did write a book, and much of it is poetry. It was my father who taught me to expect that, when you read a phrase like "thus saith the Lord," what follows that phrase is likely going to be high and lofty poetic expression.

And when we study the examples of God's aesthetic accomplishments, if we really study them, we can derive the basics of a sound aesthetic understanding. We see that skill is involved, and balance, and symmetry, and repetition, and complexity, not excluding simplicity, alliteration, and so on.

God inspired the book of Romans. We know what truth is. God gave us the Ten Commandments. So we know what goodness is. Now beauty. If you want a balanced life, you want it to reflect truth, goodness, *and beauty*.

So I Circle Back Around

You have a favorite band. Does God like your band? You have a picture hanging over your mantelpiece. Does God like it? What does Jehovah think of the photograph you selected for your computer's wallpaper?

I mean, God either likes your stuff, or He doesn't, or He doesn't care. That about exhausts all the options, right?

If God doesn't care about it, where do we get off caring about it? If God dislikes it, what business do we have liking it? But if God likes what we have done, then we may proceed with joy and exuberance.

One other thing needs to be mentioned. We do not get to make aesthetic judgments in a void, in a relativistic world—because that is a world where the only possible judgment remaining is the sneer. We want to throw up our hands in relativistic despair because "beauty is in the eye of the beholder."

We do this because if two friends start to discuss whether "God likes" something or other, and one of them is absolutely certain that God likes the Thomas Kinkaide painting that he has displayed prominently in his living room, we want to assume there is no accounting for taste. But if that is the case, then he is not wrong about his painting. A Christian critic should be able to explain what is objectively wrong with such paintings. If he can't explain it, then he has no right to a sneer.

And even a Thomas Kinkaide painting can be vastly improved with just few small embellishments. Keep that in mind.

When God evaluates a painting, let us stipulate that He likes it because of 10 million virtues He sees in it. Let us consult two critics who also like it, one with 75 reasons, and one with 28. Their lists have some areas of overlap, both with God's lists and with one another's.

Conclusion of the Matter

Once we have removed the scoffer from our midst, once we have removed the stand-alone sneer as any kind of authority, once we have eliminated the spurious distinction between high brow and low brow,

CHAPTER ELEVEN

Your Suburban Church Needed a Drum Kit the Way J.S. Bach Needed a Kazoo

On a number of different occasions, for various reasons, I have visited the sanctuaries of numerous churches. Whether there for weddings or conferences, I have often found myself in an empty meeting hall for a moment, and there, up in front, is one lonesome drum kit. And a sentiment that might reasonably spring to mind is this one: "Well, at least they tried."

But the fact that they tried doesn't keep it from being lame.

Two Distinct Issues

There are two distinct things going on, and they usually get frightfully muddled up in our debates and discussions in the "worship wars." There are, unfortunately, ecclesiastical music snobs who sneer at the drum kit being there because they regard it as a downgrade, as aiming too low. I think half the mistake is actually located in aiming too high . . . but doing so in the wrong genre.

The two issues are the *quality* of the music, evaluated according to the standards of the genre, and the *nature* of the music, evaluated according to its suitability to the occasion. In other words, if someone were to ask something like "What's wrong with this music?" the answers might range from "nothing at all" to "a great deal." But it could be entirely possible for someone to acknowledge that there was nothing wrong with the music *at all*, and to still have a huge problem with the propriety of its use in a worship service.

I admire Scott Joplin a great deal. But I still don't want *Maple Leaf Rag* used in the meditation and preparation for worship. I can object to that piece being used without objecting to the piece. I can object to the piece being used while *admiring* the piece. But then, if someone compounds our difficulty by playing *Maple Leaf Rag* and making a hash of it, we have an additional criticism. One, you shouldn't have played that song here. It doesn't really go. Secondly, if you decided to do it, you shouldn't have done it so poorly. And I say this knowing that to have done it well would actually increase some of the problems. You see this is complicated.

The musicianship displayed by a good drummer is really very high indeed. When a drummer is in the pocket, and doing well, he is *not* performing at a low level. He is performing at a high level—but if we are talking about the usual fare, and it is in church, it is in the wrong place. He is doing the wrong thing.

But then, throw this into the mix. If you have some poor church trying to fix declining attendance by getting a drum kit manned by some poor schlub who just can't do it, you find yourself not knowing where to look. Church just shouldn't be embarrassing like that.

Think of It This Way

Imagine a congregation belting out five to seven common meter tunes through the course of a worship service. Nobody is singing harmony, and the texture of the whole thing is kind of homespun. The saints are on pitch, more or less, and the acoustics in the room are decent, and so God is glorified and the congregation is edified. Despite the homespun nature of it, they are doing what Christians ought to be doing in a worship service, which is singing Psalms and hymns and spiritual songs.

Now suppose they shift over to a contemporary service. And suppose further that they get a decent drummer, and a music leader who knows his onions. They shift to a different *kind* of music, and let us say that the *quality* of the accompaniment *does* go up.

This is to say that the quality of *musicianship* can go up, while the quality of *worship* can go down. The same thing can happen in the other direction—say if the church got a pipe organ instead of drum kit. This is just to say that the saints were buried under a different kind of acoustical rock pile, the pipe organ kind instead of the rock band kind. Either way, tomayto, tomahto.

Lurking Behind

Lurking behind this whole business is the widespread evangelical assumption that music, music apart from lyrics, is merely a neutral delivery platform for whatever the lyrics might decide to say. It is simply assumed that music is not a language, and that it doesn't communicate any message of its own at all. If that were the case, it would be impossible for the music and the lyrics to be at odds with one another.

Now it is quite true that music is not a language in the sense of having verbs and direct objects, but it is false to say that music does not communicate its own independent message. For example, certain modes of music communicate mourning, and other modes of music communicate jubilation. "And saying, We have piped unto you, and ye have not danced; we have mourned unto you, and ye have not lamented" (Matt. 11:17). The music itself is not oblivious to the suitability of the occasion. The music *itself* should have something to say about where it should go.

Acceptable Worship

So the problem is not so much the kind of music people like. The problem is what kind of occasion they think a worship service is.

"Therefore let us be grateful for receiving a kingdom that cannot be shaken, and thus let us offer to God acceptable worship, with reverence and awe" (Heb. 12:28, ESV).

Because music communicates, and because we are commanded to offer God acceptable worship, and that acceptable worship is described as being offered in reverence and awe, what follows?

It follows that many congregations are offering *unacceptable* worship. They don't care about reverence and awe. When it comes to music, they refuse even to make the attempt to inculcate an atmosphere of reverence and awe. They pick songs that fight against the very concept of reverence and awe. They labor to keep everything about the service acceptable to the guy coming in off the street, who would find an atmosphere of reverence and awe stifling and off-putting.

They were told to keep our worship acceptable to the one they were (purportedly) worshiping. They do what they do instead because they are actually worshiping the potential new members, and not worshiping God.

But, we wail, what matters is the state of the heart, not the objective nature of the sacrifice. Well, actually, both matter, as we might have learned from the example of Cain. His heart was wrong, *and* his sacrifice was wrong.

We still want to maintain that the heart is all that matters, that humility is all that matters. But how is it humility to refuse even to *consider* the possibility that you are offering up to God something that He considers unacceptable worship? We don't have to pray about it because it is plainly ludicrous. Us? Unacceptable worshipers? Preposterous.

But that's not how humility rolls.

CHAPTER TWELVE

Surplices Are for Sissies

So imagine for yourself the sweetest little boy in the church, one whose mind turns naturally to edifying themes—the kind of meditative theme inspired by reflections on a porcelain figurine of the infant Samuel at prayer. Suppose further that this boy has plump cheeks, with kind of a rosy tint or glow, and those cheeks have been routinely pinched by all the pious church ladies, and they have been telling him for ever so many years that a face so cherubic should really be blessing the professors at some select seminary.

This boy is also most careful about his appearance, and in the summertime he is not to be found with his cousins gigging frogs in the swamp. He has a bookish turn, and a gentle frame. His glances turn naturally upward, to things above.

I hope it is obvious by this point in my description that the canoe of this young gentleman's masculinity is kind of wobbly in the water.

Rocking back and forth, as it were. Now imagine that the climax of this small setup is that he is eventually ordained in a communion that fits him out first thing in a white surplice. Think of that white surplice as a couple of effeminate cinder blocks thrown into that already wobbly masculinity canoe. Such an event is gonna sink that boy right to the bottom of the great pond of Gay. And please don't chafe—metaphors that don't kill us can only leave us stronger.

For those new to this mincing little deal, a surplice is a fetching little ecclesiastical number, with lacey-like accents.

For a number of centuries now, clergymen have been thought of as the third sex. There have been exceptions here and there, but the eras in which the most masculine, the most talented, the most aggressive men have been attracted to the ministry have been rare. It is far more common to have that happen with the most dutiful, the most fastidious, the most likely to have two halos in Heaven.

Getting Some Jokes Out of the Way

Jokes work for a reason, and one of those reasons is the collective wisdom of crowds. The people generally know what is going on, with "the people" defined as those who laugh. This is why jokes are often the object of various political correctness recriminations—they go right to the point, and they don't mess around.
And they are impossible to answer.

So why can't Episcopalians play chess anymore?
    They can't tell the difference between a bishop and a queen

So how do you get a nun pregnant?
    Simple. Dress her up as an altar boy.

So an archbishop was walking down the aisle of the cathedral, swinging a smoking thurible. As he passed a homosexual parishioner, the comment was, "I love your outfit, darling, but your purse is on fire."

All these jokes point to the *plain and obvious* connection between sexual deviance and a certain kind of signaling of that deviance. The problem of sexual signaling exists outside ecclesiastical circles, of course, and there are effeminate things a guy can put on that have nothing whatever to do with apostolic succession. But there has also been *a long tradition* of allowing effeminacy a place in the Church—and not only a place in the Church, but a place of honored leadership in the Church.

So . . . dress all the boys up in choir robes, with ruffs for collars, and teach them sing *beautifully*, with sweet pure tones, and surround them with a bunch of men who have no lawful sexual outlet. What could go wrong?

Some Deep Structure Here

In the religion He was founding, Jesus taught no one should be called father (Matt. 23:9-10). He prohibited disfiguring your face when you fast (Matt. 6:16). He warned against the characters who *liked* flamboyance, pointing to the nature of their bling (Matt. 23:5) and their flowing robes (Lk. 20:46). He mocked their lengthy prayers (Matt. 6:7). So there is a particular kind of showboating and parading around *that Jesus despised*. We together so far?

So it is worth pointing out that we ought not to be attracted to worship, however "historic," that embodies every last one of those things. Tall decorated hats. Elegantly styled flowing robes.

Embroidered stoles. Ash on your forehead to let everyone know you are fasting in Lent. Doing it all because the father said it was okay.

This is actually the way these things have to go. Showing off is always a sin, but it is not always an effeminate sin. But it very hard to prevent a *pious* show-off from becoming effeminate. If there was some tough guy competition, or a weight lifting competition, a guy could compete in it with all the wrong reasons, and be up to his neck in sinful show-offy motives, and yet the sin would still not be an effeminate sin. But when a man is showing off his devotion to God, or his excellence of character, or his gentleness to the poor, the mental dashboard inside somebody's head ought to be blinking *danger danger danger.*

Showing off is always diabolical. But showing off your piety is diabolical *and* gay.

So religious hypocrisy necessarily veers into effeminacy. There is a reason why sexual deviants are attracted to the Church. "And he broke down the houses of the male cult prostitutes *who were in the house of the* LORD, where the women wove hangings for the Asherah" (2 Kgs. 23:7, ESV; emphasis added).

Of course the devil wants to corrupt the church, and makes a special target of it, and that is one of the reasons these bad things happen in the church. But it also happens because when devotion to God becomes a matter of display, the whole thing is a perfect seed-bed of effeminacy. If you show off your biceps, you are just being a boor. If you show off your rotund vowels as you approach the *thaaarone of graaace*, something far worse is about to go down.

In the Luke passage cited above, Jesus doesn't castigate people for wearing robes (Lk. 20:46). Jesus wore a robe. Everybody wore a robe. Find me somebody who wasn't wearing a robe. But still He tagged it. So there were two other things going on there—*desire* and *showiness*.

"Beware of the scribes, which desire (*thelo*) to walk in long robes (*stole*), and love greetings in the markets, and the highest seats in the synagogues, and the chief rooms at feasts" (Lk. 20:46).

So when it comes to things ecclesiastical, we have to be aware of a standing temptation, ever present to a certain kind of churchman, which is the temptation to look fabulous.

Looking Like the Bride

One of the names for a prophet in Scripture is ***man of God***.

"And *there came a man of God*, and spake unto the king of Israel, and said, Thus saith the LORD, Because the Syrians have said, The LORD is God of the hills, but he is not God of the valleys, therefore will I deliver all this great multitude into thine hand, and ye shall know that I am the LORD" (1 Kgs. 20:28; emphasis added).

And this prophetic mantle is taken up in the New Testament by the minister of the Word.

"All scripture is given by inspiration of God, and is profitable for doctrine, for reproof, for correction, for instruction in righteousness: That *the man of God* may be perfect, throughly furnished unto all good works" (2 Tim. 3:16–17; emphasis added).

And not to belabor the obvious, but one of the foundational duties of every man of God is to *be a man*.

In a well-structured worship service, the people of God are meeting with their God. There is communion between them, and this communion consists of conversation. God speaks, and then we speak, and then God speaks again. We speak in the confession of sin. God speaks in the assurance of pardon. We speak in the psalm of praise. God speaks in the Scripture reading. Our congregation meets every week with God, for an hour and a half, and we talk about things with Him. He says something, and then we say something in response.

Now obviously, the Lord Jesus is not physically present with us, but He is present in the person of His Spirit. And He is also present in the office of His representative—the man of God.

When a man prays during the congregational prayer, presenting our petitions to God, he is representing the congregation to God. But when I declare the assurance of pardon to the people after we have confessed our sins, I am representing God to them. When I read the text to be preached, I am representing God to them. When I give the final benediction, I am representing God to them.

Now when a man of God is down in the front of the church discharging his office, it is crucial that he be a masculine presence there. He is supposed to be representing the groom. He has no business being down in the front of the church, looking sweet and virginal like the bride.

"But what went ye out for to see? A man clothed in soft raiment? behold, they that wear soft clothing are in kings' houses" (Matt. 11:8).

Soft raiment is always going to be a thing for somebody. But out of all the places you might be able to find it, church should be the last place you would look.

CHAPTER THIRTEEN

In Praise of America

If you can't say something *positive*, then don't say anything at all. That's what I always say. I mean to say, the world is so full of criticism and carping . . . why can't we just accentuate the positive? Focus on what is good. Try to emphasize the delightful. As Paul once put it, whatever is pure, whatever is lovely, you know. Walk on the sunny side.

Reading Their Linebackers

One of our standard practices should be to take special note of the people who are wrecking the world, and then to take another special note, a second special note as it were, of what *they* hate. When you find out what the people who are wrecking the world hate, then perhaps you have found something worthy of a defense. If you are lucky, you will have found something that is actually unpopular to defend.

I say this because the people who are wrecking the world hate America, and so I would like to rise in order to say a few things in praise of America. And I remind myself . . . no qualifications. Just praise.

Our Calvinist Constitution

One of the very best things about this nation is that we have a constitutional structure that doesn't trust Americans *at all*. People love to talk about American exceptionalism, but the really exceptional thing about our founding was that the Madisonian settlement had as its bedrock assumption the fact that human nature in America was exactly the same as it had always been throughout history, to wit, pretty grimy.

Americans have always been hustlers, on the hunt for the main chance, and so it was the sheer grace of God that the Founders devised an intricate obstacle course for them to have to get around before they would be able to start in on the eating and drinking with drunkards and beating all fellow servants.

This constitutional booby-trapping has been most necessary, what with federal judges and the EPA and all, and it hasn't worked perfectly, but boy howdy, it *has* worked. Every time the tinker-tyrants launch some new initiative, like they *always* do, whether it is to save us all from that flaming ball of fire in the sky, or to rescue the children from the opinions of their parents again, or to swoop in to define the ditch water down by your mailbox as part of the "waters of the U.S." and subject to the regulation thereof, they frequently step on another rake that was left for them on the lawn, on purpose, by James Madison himself.

So I would just like to say that a form of government that assumes total depravity in every direction is my kind of governance. I get a kind of intellectual and theological pleasure from this that starts at the ankles and gets better going up.

A Brief Interlude

Having praised our constitutional assumption of total depravity, let me proceed to a discussion of our *good* points. You say that I contradict myself? Very well, then I contradict myself; I am large, I contain multitudes. Yeah, Whitman was a weirdo, but he was very American, and that's what counts.

Where was I? Common grace is complicated, and solid cultural values can be a real thing even when the heart is deceitfully wicked.

Americans Are Ebullient

This country is a cheerful can-do place. The Construction Battalion of the Navy (the Seabees) had a motto that epitomizes this attitude nicely: "The difficult we do now, the impossible takes a little longer."

During the Second World War, we built a fleet of Liberty Ships, thousands of them. We got to the point where we were churning out three a day. And, at one point, apparently just to prove that it could be done, one shipyard built one of them, keel to masts, in *one* day.

And on top of that kind of thing, I can't do something as simple as going into McDonald's for a cheeseburger without being reminded of my responsibility to have a good day.

Do it right, do it now, all my fellow citizens tell me. And do it while having a nice day.

Some of our people were residing in another country a few years back, and the locals Christians were complaining about the education options, which were admittedly poor. "So why don't you start a school?" our people asked, innocently enough. The response really should have been anticipated. "That is just so *American*."

Starting something is American?

So America is to the world what Texas is to America. Now you sometimes might want to make sure to watch your dosages carefully, because too much might be kind of like a bit of Mulliner's Buck-U-Uppo. Please take note of the literary allusion. I am quoting a British writer, but one who was very fond of Americans.

Americans Are Generous

Routinely upbraided for being selfish and piggy, Americans are actually the most generous people on the planet. I am not referring to the lunatic behavior of whoever is behind our foreign aid daisy cutter approach, but rather to the rivers of private charity.

Whenever a humanitarian disaster happens, from a tsunami to a hurricane to an earthquake, thousands and thousands of $20 donations make their way into the relief. And by every measurement, Americans are way down the road ahead of everyone else in this.

You can almost consider it a law. There is an inverse relationship between the actual generosity of a group and the reputation it has with the cool kids *for* generosity. The most generous people in the world are Americans. The most generous Americans are religious Americans. Among religious Americans, the most generous are Protestants. Among the Protestants, the most generous are the evangelicals. Using another grid, Arthur Brooks showed years ago that the most generous state in the Union, as indicated by private donations of every kind, was . . . wait for it . . . Mississippi. The *least* generous was either Connecticut or Massachusetts, I forget which. Does it matter?

Generosity takes many forms. I am also talking about the many thousands of Americans leaving the richest country in the history of the world in order to give it all away on the mission field. These are individual choices, obviously, but they arise out of shared cultural values.

And this would obviously include the recent martyrdom of John Allen Chau. To paraphrase the words of the great missionary John Paton, the fact that he shed his blood there means that this island will most certainly be secured for Christ.

It also provides us with a standing reminder of how self-absorbed Internet observers can get away with chiding him for his "selfish" death. Yeah, that's the ticket. Love is hate. Selfishness is altruism. Sacrifice must be the real selfishness.

Actually, a big part of real selflessness is budgeting for all the people who reserve their right to keep a safe distance from every form of authentic Christian living. If it "fails," they can sniff and say they didn't really approve, and if it succeeds they can rally around afterwards for the awards ceremonies. They *are* the one talent and they bury themselves in the napkin.

Generosity is as generosity does.

Americans Know How to Fight

We cannot leave this subject without praising American combativeness. When a fight is necessary, and the need for it has finally become obvious, one of the things you want by your side in a dark alley, bricks at your back, is an American.

During the American Civil War, a Yankee was speaking about the war over in Manchester, England. The crowd was a hostile one because Manchester was a textile town that had had a relationship

with the South because of the cotton. Anyway, the crowd was giving this Yankee a hard time because of how long the war was taking.
Initial predictions had been that it would be a matter of weeks.
One of the hecklers jeered that subduing the South sure was taking
a long *time*, wasn't it, a lot longer than predicted? Yes, the speaker
allowed. It was taking a lot longer than we had anticipated. What we
should have factored into the equation was the fact that we would
be fighting Americans.

A Flash of Self-Awareness

I do know, and do not need to be further informed, that I am a very
American writer.

CHAPTER FOURTEEN

In Hell Where They Already Have It

The title comes from an old line of Ronald Reagan's, where he said, *"Socialism* only works in two places: Heaven where *they* don't *need it* and *hell where they already have it."*

Let that suffice for a rudimentary introduction, setting both tone and direction.

So Lay the Axe at the Root

Socialism is, at root, not a math problem. It is an envy problem, with math splotches on the skin. Socialism is not an economics problem. It is an envy problem, with a symptomatic swelling of the economic lymph nodes. Socialism is not a political problem. It is an envy problem, with a few skirmishes over who has to pay for the political motorized wheel chair. Those subsidized wheelchairs are advertised, incidentally, on Fox News, bastion of opposition to government handouts.

Socialism is, at the heart, a disease of the heart. It is a *spiritual* problem.

As such, the problem cannot be solved in a math class, or a course in sound economics. The problem can be solved there in theory, on *paper* ("See? You cannot spend what you have not earned." "*Ooohhh . . .*"). But solving the problem on paper is not the same thing as solving the problem.

Upton Sinclair, an outspoken socialist, at least understood the principle—or at least when it applied to others. He said, "It is difficult to get a man to understand something, when his salary depends on his not understanding it."

Isn't that the way? We all understand the problems with *other* people's socialism. Margaret Thatcher made the famous quip about the problem with socialism being the fact that "sooner or later, you run out of other people's money." This is exactly true, but we also have to deal with the fact that many Americans are afraid of other people's socialism, but not at all bothered by their own. Ostensible conservatives have completely rolled over on any number of socialistic programs (e.g. government education), and have quietly acquiesced on others, albeit with some grumbling (e.g. Social Security). But whether or not you think it is politically feasible to address the problems with any form of economic redistribution (which is simple theft, fueled by envy), the envy is still there, doing its destructive work.

Because this is not an intellectual problem, because it is a spiritual disease, there is only one possible solution—and that is the cross of the Lord Jesus, the place where all envy must go to die.

How Is Socialism Envious?

I began with the assertion. Here is the argument.

You have heard a great deal about the nefarious 1%—you know, those fat cats who look like that top hatted guy on the Monopoly board? Those slick daddies who are suffocating all us ordinary people with their toxic, greasy, smoky greed? Let me kick start the envy part of this discussion.

In our country, that top 1% earned about 20% of all the income earned. Boo, hiss, right? Income inequality is thought to be such a terrible thing.

But out of the total amount of taxes *paid*, that same group paid about 40% of them. The bottom 50% of our population paid about 2.7% of all the tax revenues. The remainder, and a big remainder it is (97.3%) was paid by the top 50%. Slice it up another way and you discover that the top 1% pay more taxes (around 40%) than *all* the taxpayers in the entire bottom 90% combined (around 30%). And then, if you want to compare tax *rates*, the top 1% pay an average rate of 27%, which is more than seven times greater than the average rate paid by the taxpayers in the bottom 50%.[13]

Now glance over those figures again. And then reflect on the fact that we live in a country, in a time—shoot, let's just call it a fun house—where it is possible for a politician to stand up in the broad light of day in order to *opine* that it is *his* opinion that the rich need to be made to pay their fair share. Not only can he do this, but he can do this without being laughed out of public life forever.

Fair share? Stop saying fair share. Give us a *number*. When will we have arrived at a truly equitable solution? What is the mystical number that constitutes an actual fair share? The answer, of course, is when all the plain girls are pretty, and all the figs trees are dropping their diamonds on the ground. The answer, my friend, is blowing in the wind.

13. See here: https://taxfoundation.org/summary-latest-federal-income-tax-data -2016-update/

This is spiritual blindness. It is spiritual stupor. It is judicial stupidity. It is heart disease.

If someone is in the grip of this delusion, and you try to fix it by going over math facts with him, you are healing the wound lightly. And besides, he probably did better in math back in school than you did. *That* is not the problem.

The Economics of the Cross

Socialists want the right to want absolutely anything that belongs to others. They disguise what they are doing by pretending they want it for others, taking from the rich to give to the poor, but that is not what is going on at bottom. They want it for themselves, and they want it now. They have a permanent case of the gimmees.

But I do need to correct one thing.

There is *one* thing belonging to another that they really don't want. They don't want the *righteousness* that belongs to another. They want a free lunch, not free grace.

And so here is the basic alternative. I have said it before, and will say again as many times as they will let me. Here it is: free grace > free men > free markets. You cannot get to the third in any kind of sustained way without the second, and you cannot ever get the second without the first.

So what does that mean? It means that atheist libertarians are a big part of the problem. That's one thing. Another is that Christian communitarians are the other part. The libertarians love apple harvests while hating orchards. The communitarians love the trees but hate the fruit.

Either men will cry out for free grace, or they will cry out for free lunches.

If you will not have the grace of God on His terms, then you will try to supply your counterfeit version of grace by pouring out your largesse on the people. But of course, unlike God, who is rich and abounding in whatever He gives by nature, we have to *steal* what we give. Thomas Sowell put it like this: "The welfare state is the oldest con game in the world. First you take people's money away quietly and then you give some of it back to them flamboyantly."

I said earlier that the cross of Christ is where envy must go if it is to die. And it must die if all the follies that proceed from it are to die. The reason the rising generation is so attracted to socialism, the wasting disease of the entire twentieth century, has been primarily a failure of *evangelism*.

The fact that all our gospel-centered this n' thatism has missed this point should be a grief and embarrassment to us.

CHAPTER FIFTEEN

In Defiance of the Schoolmarms

I do indeed intend to defy the schoolmarms, but you will pardon me if I take a few minutes to set the whole thing up first.

In the twelfth chapter of Acts, just a few verses apart, Luke gives us two instances of the angel of the Lord striking somebody, but with very different results.

> And, behold, the angel of the Lord came upon him, and a light shined in the prison: and he smote Peter on the side, and raised him up, saying, Arise up quickly. And his chains fell off from his hands. (Acts 12:7)

> And immediately the angel of the Lord smote [Herod], because he gave not God the glory: and he was eaten of worms, and gave up the ghost. (Acts 12:23)

In both instances, we have the angel of the Lord. The same verb for striking is used in both instances (*patasso*). Both instances occur in the presence of some sort of glory. With Peter, light shone in the prison. With Herod, he was arrayed in royal splendor. In both cases, the angel struck the middle of the body. We are told that the angel hit Peter on the side, and with Herod we can conclude from the fact that he was eaten by worms that the angel struck him somewhere in the middle.

There is little doubt in my mind that Luke is having fun with this, but we must also recognize that the point of all the parallels is to make a contrast that was the fundamental point. The striking was the *deliverance* of Peter, and the *destruction* of Herod. Note that again—the point of all the parallels was to make a contrast.

Making a Right Judgment

In rhetoric, the point of stasis theory is to teach the student to identify what is in fact the main point, the hinge upon which everything turns, and not to be distracted by various extraneous issues. Nothing is worse than watching someone debate one of the bad guys, the trunk of whose tree is open and exposed, with a chain saw sitting on the ground by that trunk, quietly idling, and *then* to have his orthodox interlocutor take off down the street, chasing some of the stray leaves that the wind blew off.

The Lord told us to use our heads and hearts together when we make an assessment. "Judge not according to the appearance, but judge righteous judgment" (Jn 7:24).

Deciding the right thing to do should be straightforward. But that is not the same thing as saying that it is simple in a cookie-cutter kind of way. To most of the saints at Antioch, Paul was creating an unnecessary controversy over the seating arrangements at the potluck.

But Paul knew that unless he threw down at that point, the gospel itself would be compromised (Gal. 2:11). David ate the showbread and was justified (Matt. 12:4), while Uzzah just tried to prevent the ark of the covenant from tipping over and was slain for his efforts (2 Sam. 6:6). It would have been a terrible compromise to acquiesce in the circumcision of Titus (Gal. 2:3), and it was no compromise at all to have Timothy circumcised (Acts 16:3).

In absolutely every situation that contains more than two variables, those variables can always be rearranged in such a way as to tell a story that is direct *opposite* of the story that God wants you to derive from it. After all of Jeremiah's melancholy prophecies had been fulfilled, after his *bona fides* as a true prophet of God had been triply proved, there were some who had the effrontery to say all these disasters had befallen Jerusalem because they had not worshiped the Queen of Heaven *enough* (Jer. 44:18). Yeah, that's the ticket.

That's our story, they said, and we're sticking to it.

The ChapStick Incident

So let me tell you a story. Quite a few years ago now, my two daughters were giving a presentation to a number of young college girls. One of the points they were communicating to the girls, among others, was that Christian women should be responsible for policing the boundaries of their own personal spaces, and that they should not allow any of the brothers to encroach uninvited.

One of my girls used an example from back in her college days, where a friend had grabbed a tube of her ChapStick, used it, whereupon he then attempted to return it. She had refused to take it back on the principle that she was not going to allow *him* to unilaterally determine whether or not things like that were okay with her.

So then, girls, the point of the exhortation was to show young women how not to be manipulated by men, whether in great things or small. We should all be for that, right?

This was many years ago. But there was a vocal cohort of point-missers among the girls present ("I can't believe she said friends can't share ChapStick if they want."). The point they thought they had heard rapidly assumed the proportions of an outrage, and so the story has been passed down to subsequent generations of girls. "There are ChapStick legalists out there . . . ware! ware!"

Now the problem is this. The young ladies who missed the point are actually the kind of women who, if a married friend finally had to resort to the desperate measure of getting a restraining order against a brutal husband, would be the very first to mount the Facebook barricades to demand that the entire world respect her choices, respect her space, respect her privacy. Fine. Good. Great, in fact.

But if someone proposes equipping such women *earlier* in life on how to recognize such things early on, and how to respond to such things when they are relatively simple, and not so devastating—no dice, Pharisee.

So Then, to the Schoolmarms

Schoolmarms usually know something, but it is generally limited in scope, and runs on a narrow gauge track. They know their subject, and their immediate duties. But they do not know the world. They do not know how their subject fits into the larger world because in their minds, their subject of choice *is* the world.

The adage has, in their case, been fulfilled in a most illuminating way. When all you have is a hammer, every problem looks like a nail.

A schoolmarm is fastidious, and couples this with having no sense of place or proportion.

Their thing might be Latin, or it might be music, or it might be health and fitness, or it might networking on behalf of friends who have had to take out restraining orders, or it might be activism against apostrophe abuse, or it might be classical Christian education, or it might be all about the importance of the Oxford comma, or some other cause for the true-hearted. The operations of this true believer, which are usually destructive, might occur in a school, in a corporation, in a church office, in a college, or in a family—they are willing to destroy the harmony of whatever host they might be inhabiting.

When one thing is treated as though it were the *only* thing, conflict is usually not very far away. This conflict can happen with rival aspiring empires because there is the football team, chess club, and the music program, and your kid can't do them all, and a representative of each one has hold of your kid's leg, and both arms.

Conflict can also happen when people with normal balanced lives kick at the unreasonable demands being placed on them.

Not only is there conflict, but their fastidious pursuit of what they have hoicked up into the rafters of the sublime frequently results in the destruction of the thing they pretend to admire so much.

Dorothy Sayers and C.S. Lewis both described how the purists of the Latin restoration movement in the Renaissance succeeded only in destroying Latin. There was one guy, floating above the common herd, who refused to use any Latin form that could not be reproduced from Cicero. By arbitrarily defining Periclean Athens and Augustan Rome as the high water mark, as establishing what had to be treated as *the* standard, they succeeded only in destroying the use of Latin as a living language. For if Latin were to be a living language, there would have to be a way of saying *jogging*, or *toaster oven*, or *iPhone* in it. That just seems so . . . tacky. Not the kind of thing a purist wants to do. What if you went into the grocery store and in aisle 13 your child cries out, *Ecce! Ursuli gummi!* Your eyes narrow because the Latin teacher has apparently been fooling around.

Schoolmarms are experts in making the perfect the enemy of the good. More specifically, they make the perfect *one* thing the enemy of the balanced *many* things.

Two Last Things

Specialists are most necessary, but the model needs to be a Pauline one. It is a body life thing, and there are two aspects to this. There are two ways for a person to give himself to the pursuit of excellence in his chosen vocation, and to do so without raining mayhem down on the heads of all others. There are two ways, in other words, to avoid becoming a schoolmarm in whatever subject it is you have chosen. And what is it that you have become instead of becoming a schoolmarm? Let's call it becoming a ninja. For a ninja, *balance* is everything.

The first is to realize, accept, and love the fact that the emphasis that others place on things that leave you utterly uninterested is an emphasis that God gave them. God wants the liver to want to do things that the ankles, and eyes, and kidneys have no desire whatever to do. This is the *fact* of body life (1 Cor. 12:16-17).

And the second thing is learning to render to those with other gifts what you (in your better moments) wish they would render to you in your pursuits. If you wish they would recognize the value of what you do, then start by recognizing the value of what they do. This is the law and the prophets (Phil. 2:3). This is qualitative love and humility in that body life.

And it sets us free to pursue excellence in what God has given to us without becoming a fastidious pain in the neck. Don't do that. Being a pain in the neck does not count as body life.

CHAPTER SIXTEEN

Mere Hellfire

The doctrine of eternal punishment is one that is widely known, or at least the broad outline of the doctrine is widely known. That is, if you were to ask the average person what "Hell" is, they would be able to reply that it was the purported place of punishment in the afterlife. And this is correct, as far as it goes. The problem is that this doesn't go very far in describing something that goes on forever.

The Simple Fact of It

Despite the best attempts of our new gangs of exegetical ameliorators—men who walk around the perimeters of the doctrine of damnation with Greek word study spritzer bottles, trying to cool it off a bit—the teaching of Scripture on the final and ultimate wrath of God remains what it has always been—plain, obvious, and undeniable.

Wherefore if thy hand or thy foot offend thee, cut them off, and cast them from thee: it is better for thee to enter into life halt or maimed, rather than having two hands or two feet *to be cast into everlasting fire.* (Matt. 18:8; emphasis added throughout)

And whosoever was not found written in the book of life was *cast into the lake of fire.* (Rev. 20:15)

Enter ye in at the strait gate: for wide is the gate, and broad is the way, *that leadeth to destruction*, and many there be which go in thereat. (Matt. 7:13)

What if God, willing to shew his wrath, and to make his power known, endured with much longsuffering the *vessels of wrath fitted to destruction.* (Rom. 9:22)

He that believeth on the Son hath everlasting life: and he that believeth not the Son shall not see life; but *the wrath of God abideth on him.* (Jn. 3:36)

And there are many other passages in Scripture to the same effect, and all of them as gray as cold steel.

If God had wanted the Church to come to a conclusion that some very pleasant destiny awaits us all, and that a quiet annihilation was to be the fate of the very worst, then surely He sought to inculcate this doctrine among us in a strange, roundabout, and counterproductive way. If you don't want people thinking that their destiny could include being eaten by worms everlastingly, then why warn them about the place where the worm does not die (Mark 9:44)? If you don't want them thinking in terms of eternal fire, then why did you bring the eternal fire up (Matt. 25:41)? If you didn't want people thinking of Hell as a place where you might be carried, bound hand and foot, then why use illustrations involving those who were bound hand and foot (Matt. 22:13)?

So we begin with the plain fact of Hell. Hell is an expression of the final and complete outpouring of God's wrath on human unbelief and rebellion. Since the Fall of man, the condition of being under that wrath is humanity's baseline condition. If a man does not believe, then the wrath of God remains on him (Jn. 3:36). Before we come to faith, we are by nature objects of wrath, just as the others (Eph. 2:3). We do not need to achieve damnation; we are damned already. We may, by the grace of Christ, *escape* damnation, but this is a very different thing, as we will see shortly.

Inexcusable

The word *inexcusable* occurs twice in the New Testament, both places in the early part of Romans. When we say that something is *inexcusable*, we mean that it is really bad—awful. The Greek word for it is *anapologetos*, and the apostle Paul uses it twice—once in Romans 1 and then again in Romans 2.

In the first instance, he says that those who live lives of moral defiance, in the light of what every man knows about God and His character from the creation, and whether they admit it or not, are men who are "without excuse" (Rom. 1:20). In the second instance, Paul argues that men are without excuse because they judge other men according to a standard they refuse to live by themselves (Rom. 2:1).

So the two things that are inexcusable according to Paul are, first, refusal to live by what God declares through natural revelation in creation, and second, insistence upon applying that same standard to other people. "Natural revelation can't tell *me* what to do, and this same natural revelation is most certainly binding on *you*."

This iniquitous approach to moral standards—binding for thee, but not for me—is sufficient to secure a righteous and holy damnation for every mother's son of us.

Suppose God had an invisible digital recorder that hangs around every person's neck. This is one high-tech digital recorder in that it only records moral condemnations of *other* people, whenever we happen to make them. "I can't believe he promised . . ." "That was a gross violation of trust . . . ." "That slut . . . ."

Suppose further that God takes these recordings, and from each one He derives a moral code to live by, and this code is made up entirely of the demands we made upon other people. And then, as the Day of Judgment arrives, He determines to judge each one of us by that code. Will any of us fare any better if it were to be done this way? Not a bit of it. All of us, every one of us, would be damned to Hell on the simple basis of what we said everyone else ought to be doing. In short, we would all be condemned to Hell on the basis of our *inexcusable* behavior—applying to absolutely everyone else what we refused to live by ourselves.

This is our condition. This is what we are *like*. This is the problem. All of us are damned in principle, and the question is whether any can be rescued from it. It is not as though we are in some in-between spot, deciding whether to go in the saved or the damned direction. We are objects of wrath *now*.

The Kind of People Who Go There

When the New Testament talks about delivering the people who are headed down to the dust of death, it does not deal in things like baptism, or singing in the choir, or the legacy of a godly family, or getting them to homeschool, or baking whole grain breads, or eating healthy, or engaging with culture. It talks about the cross of Jesus Christ, and by this I do not mean the cross of Jesus Christ used as though you were warding off vampires.

Many years ago I was talking to a young woman, and I asked her about the gospel. Her answers were solid—catechism pure. I asked for gospel and I heard gospel repeated back. But then I asked her where she would go if she dropped dead right then. "Oh, I would go to Heaven," she said. "Why?" I asked. "Oh, I am a good person. I sing in the choir. I work with 4-H."

The default mode of the sinful human heart is to trust in *self.* This self-trust can be decorated in any number of ways, some of them orthodox, but when it comes down to the point the trust is in self. This is even the case when that self is riddled with the kind of corruptions that Scripture tells us is *not* going to inherit the kingdom.

"Now the works of the flesh are manifest, which are these; Adultery, fornication, uncleanness, lasciviousness, idolatry, witchcraft, hatred, variance, emulations, wrath, strife, seditions, heresies, envyings, murders, drunkenness, revellings, and such like: of the which I tell you before, as I have also told you in time past, that *they which do such things shall not inherit the kingdom of God*" (Gal. 5:19–21; emphasis added).

"Know ye not that the unrighteous *shall not inherit the kingdom of God?* Be not deceived: neither fornicators, nor idolaters, nor adulterers, nor effeminate, nor abusers of themselves with mankind, nor thieves, nor covetous, nor drunkards, nor revilers, nor extortioners, *shall inherit the kingdom of God*" (1 Cor. 6:9–10; emphasis added).

So what kind of people—baptized-and-in-the-Church people— are *not* going to inherit the kingdom of God? What kind of people clean up on the outside real nice when they go to church, but inside they are full of dead men's bones? They are Christians of a sort, in that they obviously belong to the visible Church, and are equally obviously part of the covenant, but what sort of Christian are they? They are the kind who are going to Hell.

Greedy businessman Christian. Motel porn Christian. Sharp dealer Christian. Foul mouthed Christian. Effeminate Christian. Quarrelsome Christian. Envy-ridden Christian. Nightclub scene Christian. False accuser on the Internet Christian. And also keep in mind that it is possible for someone to be in the Christian scene and thus prevented from doing any of these things in a flamboyant way, doing them anonymously, or secretly, or internally, and yet be the kind of person who keeps all of these sorts of sins as a morsel under his tongue. He thinks of them when he rises up, when he walks along the road, and when he lies down.

"Incline not my heart to any evil thing, to practise wicked works with men that work iniquity: and let me not eat of their dainties" (Ps. 141:4).

The Nature of Symbols

So a lot of evangelical Christians are Hell-bound. This is where a large part of the exegetical energy to find a "way of escape" is coming from. One of those escapes is to learn that much of the final eschatological language of Scripture is "symbolic." *Whew!* That was a close one!

Now it is quite true that the final wrath of God is described for us under various figures, some of which seem to us to conflict with each other, or to somehow be in tension. How can a lake of fire be an outer darkness? How can eternal pain be a final destruction?

When we use symbolic language to describe a great thing, we must always keep in mind the fact that the symbol is always *less* than the reality. What is greater—the nation or the flag that represents that nation? Of course the nation is the represented reality, and is obviously the greater. What is greater—the marriage or the ring on the finger that represents the marriage? Of course the marriage is the represented reality, and is obviously much greater than a small piece of metal.

If the language representing Hell to us in Scripture is literal, then it is a terrible place to be. If the language representing Hell to us is symbolic, that that means the reality is far, far worse than that. If it is symbolic, then that means the images of "excruciating pain forever" are a small attempt to get at something so appalling that the unenlightened mind collapses in horror.

When we understand the language, it is clear Scripture *intends* for us to recoil in horror. Left out of the reasonable responses would be an interpretation of damnation that is actually pretty close to the Buddhist view of salvation. Annihilation is close enough to Nirvana for government work. No good reading of the text can elicit a response *opposite* that which was clearly intended by the text.

Beer and All My Friends

Another response is to try to brazen it out. Unbelievers do this openly, but the unbelieving heart inside the Church will attempt some variant of it, at least. Who of us has not heard unbelievers putting off this ultimate question off with a lame joke and an even lamer laugh. "Oh, I don't mind going to Hell. All my friends will be there." Or "Why wouldn't I want to go to Hell? That's where all the beer is going to be."

Friendship? In the outer darkness? Unless you can become friends with the eternal echoes of your own petulant voice, there are no friends there. There is no such thing as friendship or companionship *at all* any more, and all the beer is going to be in Heaven.

We are an insolent and slick generation. When unbelievers talk about the afterlife their great stumper question for us is "how can a just God send people to Hell?" We truly have inverted right and wrong, sweet and bitter, up and down (Is. 5:20). The problem of Hell presents no problem to the justice of God whatsoever, and the reason for this is the fact that Hell is nothing *but* the justice of God. The problem for God's justice was presented by the reality of Heaven for sinners, and that very real problem required a crucifixion to solve.

We are given no indication in Scripture that your former friends and loved ones will be looking on as you are condemned, bound, and dragged off. But if they are, you can be assured that they will have no trouble with the just sentence of God that has been pronounced over you. Their faces will be pitiless, and that will be as it should be. There is one place in the entire New Testament where the saints of God cry out, "Hallelujah," and that is when they are watching the smoke of Babylon's destruction ascend into the sky forever and ever (Rev. 19:3). Perhaps this is why we are told to have pity now on those who are perishing. A time is coming when pity is the last thing a righteous soul would ever want to extend.

And when you are bound and carried off, you will not be delivered in the midst of the fiery furnace the way Shadrach, Meshach, and

Abednego were. And the angels who carry you there will not be consumed themselves, the way Nebuchadnezzar's men were. And God's anger with you will never cool down, the way Nebuchadnezzar's did.

In salvation, there will be no more tears—every tear will be wiped away (Rev. 21:4). In Hell, there will be weeping and gnashing of teeth (Matt. 8:12). In Hell, it is *right* that there be weeping and gnashing of teeth. It requires no apology from Heaven, or from the company of the redeemed. It is not that we believe in the doctrine of eternal damnation, but are suitably sheepish about it. A heartfelt apology *is* owed, but from the damned, which they absolute refuse to give, which is why they are damned.

What You Are Becoming

Everyone in the world is in the process of becoming someone. Salvation is the process of being increasingly conformed to the image of the Lord Jesus Christ—becoming an actual *someone*, becoming a real human being. Damnation is the final descent into an inchoate, disintegrated agonistic whine—having insisted through long years that the self be simultaneously left alone and also promoted to the level of importance it deserves. That self finally receives the fruition of that demand, and achieves its ultimate deserved value, which is zero. They received what they demanded, and it included leanness to the soul (Ps. 106:15).

Viewing the Game Film

So by all our reckoning, November was a success. What I thought I would do here is report back to you on a few of the relevant stats, in order to evaluate things by that metric, and then spend a few additional moments on the only metric that ultimately matters.

The Crowd That Came

"In the mean time, when there were gathered together an innumerable multitude of people, insomuch that they trode one upon another . . . ."(Lk. 12:1)

Compared to the same period in 2017, my blog traffic was up 51%. New users increased by 63%, so that's all good. That infamous burning couch video racked up some successes of its own. That video was viewed on Facebook, YouTube and Twitter just shy of

110K times, presumably with some people watching more than once in order to silently exhort me to talk faster. It is safe to say that the video got around. And as the capstone of all this activity, we were able to give away over 60K copies of the free e-books (for the sake of precision, there were 60,824 downloads). All in all, November was a time in which we were able to get the word out. Thank you all for your part in making it work.

The Crowd That Didn't Show

There are three kinds of people who don't read my stuff. The first category, by far the largest, is made up of the people who have never heard of me. This number, speaking frankly between us girls, almost runs into the double digit billions, and includes all the principalities and powers.

The second category is made up of those worthies who do know who I am, and who have occasionally read my work, usually when an eager relative emails it to them. But for whatever reason, the timbre of my writing, not to mention the shape of my head, is not their cup of tea. They agree with what I am saying, for the most part, but my manner of expression is not how they speak or write, and so they can take it or leave it. In this category I would also include those pastors who have parishioners who are super-fans of mine, and who have needed extra measures of grace from God to reply charitably whenever they are informed, after every third sermon or so, that "Doug Wilson says something different." To such pastors, I can only say that you have my deepest regards, and I know.

But the third category—this is the category of the arch and distant. This is the person who frequently reads me but who thinks it is important (for various reasons) not ever to say so. On the one end, this category over the years has actually included many friends. I don't know how many times someone has written me to commend me for a particular post, and they will introduce the commendation with "I don't actually read your blog, but . . ." That was good, but don't get a big head. We hate it when people get big heads. That kind of thing, at least for me on the receiving end, is spiritually healthy and bracing.

In the middle are the secret fans, the people who would retweet stuff if the enforcers would leave them alone, but the enforcers never leave them alone. We can see how this works from time to time. Say that somebody with a significant Twitter following slips the leash and retweets something about me or from me. Immediately the sibilant silencers surround that offending tweet, whacking away at it like it was a baby seal. "sssssitler . . . ssssslavery . . . raaaacccccccism . . ."

But then on the other end, on the important end, we find the Serious Persons. These are the people running the evangelical embargo against all things Moscow. I must not be mentioned, and I must not be mentioned for reasons of state. They don't ever want to be put in the position where I have been maintaining something straight out of Deuteronomy, say, and then they are asked, with cameras running, if they agree with that. To agree would set the cat among the media pigeons, and to disagree would set a different cat among some very different donor pigeons.

So these are the people who are very aware of who I am and what I am doing, and they consider it a significant threat to their project, which is to keep the prospects for their project shiny and unbesmirched. Mentioning me is not a good way to do that. I am not a great traveling companion for those who would arrive at their destination unbesmirched.

A case in point? Shall I give you a case in point? From O. Alan Noble: "But for real, the best thing we can do for Doug Wilson is stop reading him, stop treating him as a Serious Person, and pray for him and those under his influence."[14]

Oh, but, it must be said, I have no desire whatever to be a Serious Person. That is the problem of our era—all these Serious Persons. Seriously? Who actually wants to be a Serious Person? We have forgotten the warning from Chesterton: "Without education, we are in a horrible and deadly danger of taking educated people seriously."

I do want to take the truth seriously, and I do want to be a serious threat to a certain kind of pomposity, the kind that has filled out the ranks of our evangelical leadership. But being a serious threat requires, almost by definition, that you not care about being a Serious Person. "How can ye believe, which receive honour one of another, and seek not the honour that cometh from God only?" (Jn 5:44).

So there were various reasons for hosting this No Quarter November–some of them experimental, and others that were simply making more of a statement. I do not need to go into all of that here, but one of the statements is this one. If the success of an embargo is measured by actually stopping the flow of goods stored in the holds of smugglers' ships, then November was a bad month for the embargo, and a good month for the smugglers.

14 O. Alan Noble (@TheAlanNoble), Twitter, December 2, 2018, 12:53 p.m., https://twitter.com/TheAlanNoble/status/1069333863011373056.